S0-AQM-734

BUSINESS INTELLIGENCE
Putting It All Together

Kirk W. M. Tyson

Leading Edge Publications

Printed in the United States of America

First Printing: December 1986

Library of Congress Cataloging in Publication Data

Tyson, Kirk W. M.
Business Intelligence.

        Includes index.
        1. Competitor Intelligence   I. Title
        2. Strategic Planning
HD38.7.T95   1986   658.4'7   86-27309
ISBN 0-941101-00-2

In memory of
Dr. Kimon Bournazos
A man who believed that anything could
be achieved with a little persistence.

Contents

Figures

Exhibits

Appendices

Preface

This book has evolved over many years. Business Intelligence is not a revolutionary concept. It has been around for quite some time. But most companies have just come to realize over the last few years that a more formalized system of business intelligence will be necessary for survival in the 1990s.

A few research firms have attempted in the past to discuss the topic of business intelligence. Unfortunately, they approached the subject from a research point of view rather than a planning point of view. It is in the strategic and tactical planning processes where the true value of intelligence is realized. I hope this book fills the void left by others.

My objectives for this book are to:

- Communicate the necessity for business intelligence

- Provide an understanding of the overall business intelligence methodology

- Discuss various alternatives for conducting intelligence activities

- Provide a framework for developing an on-going system of continuous monitoring

I will discuss the use of effective legal techniques for obtaining information about competitors, customers and suppliers as well as how to analyze data and synthesize it into meaningful "action oriented" reports. I will describe how to set up an effective system to tap the most valuable intelligence sources. Finally, I will discuss how to protect the secrets of your own organization.

I would like to thank several people who have assisted in this effort. First I would like to thank my wife, Kathie, for her overall support. Secondly I would like to recognize the employees of my firm who put up with the "do not disturb" signs on my door and ran the business in my absence. All of these people were helpful in the final editing stages.

I would also like to thank Dr. Brian Long who provided valuable advice and counsel in the writing of this book and the production of associated video programs.

Finally, I would like to thank the hundreds of clients with whom I've been associated over the years for providing me with many war stories and alternative approaches to intelligence gathering.

Kirk W. M. Tyson
Oak Brook, Illinois

BUSINESS INTELLIGENCE
Putting It All Together

Introduction

We thought it was interesting when the Japanese came over to this country armed with their camera equipment. We thought it was interesting that they were taking pictures of everything in sight. We said to ourselves, "How cute."

We didn't realize that the Japanese were conducting business intelligence activities on a massive scale. We saw them in department stores, in manufacturing plants and many other places taking pictures of machinery, equipment, products, store fixtures and displays. They used these pictures and other information to develop their overall plans for Japanese enterprise. We all know how tremendously successful they were.

We encounter business intelligence activities almost daily but don't realize it. How many times have you visited a grocery store and seen people with hand-held calculators standing by the racks of merchandise? As many as 25% of these people are not taking inventory nor are they store employees. They are employees of competing companies whose products are displayed on the shelves. Their function is to gather and record information about products and prices.

These are examples of how business intelligence has been historically conducted. Unfortunately many managers don't realize how widespread the practice of business intelligence has become over the last few years. It is now practiced in almost every industry.

Fortunately, it is not too late to develop your own business intelligence system. A recent review of the current "state-of-the-art" of business intelligence systems found many serious flaws in the techniques and approaches currently employed:

■ Most companies use only the most common trade sources for obtaining intelligence and the chosen sources generally yield little value.

■ Unrealistic expectations have slowed the intelligence activities of most companies.

In addition, many company managers have difficulty relating the cost of conducting intelligence activities to the benefits received. For these and other reasons, business intelligence is still evolving as an integral management function.

Some people perceive intelligence activities as a wartime or cold war activity. Certainly the benefit of intelligence activities is clearly seen in the military area. The largest naval battle fought, the battle of Midway Island in World War II, was won by the United States not because the United States had a superior force but because of its intelligence efforts. The United States was able to crack enough of the Japanese code to determine their intention to attack Midway Island. The Japanese lost the element of surprise.

Similarly, business intelligence should be an early warning system — a system that alerts a company to a competitor's impending move or helps to determine how a competitor will respond to **your** company's moves. Rarely does this level of intelligence require "perfect vision." A few key pieces of information can make the strategic difference.

Unfortunately, the word "intelligence" conjures up images of illegal or unethical activities. Clearly, companies do not need to use practices such as phone tapping or bribing to gather information.

In his book, *Secret Mission; The Story of An Intelligence Officer,* World War II Navy Captain Ellis Zacharias observed that in peacetime the Navy derived its information from three sources in these proportions:

■ 95% from public sources

■ 4% from semi-public sources

■ 1% or less from secret sources

Captain Zacharias further wrote, "There is very little these confidential agents can tell that is not accessible to an alert analyst who knows what he is looking for and knows how to find it in open sources." Like naval information, business information is generally available in the public sphere if you know where to find it and how to get it.

Don't let the intrigue of industrial espionage cause you to stray from your real reason for gathering, analyzing and utilizing intelligence. The real reason is to help your company achieve competitive advantage. Unscrupulous techniques are too dangerous and costly compared to the amount of information derived from them.

Continuous monitoring of competitors, customers, suppliers and other industry forces should be an integral part of the overall strategic management function for every company. Continuous monitoring prevents a company from being surprised. By keeping apprised of industry developments, a company can take appropriate and timely strategic action.

Although the moves of significant companies may be painfully obvious, the move of a seemingly insignificant company in the marketplace can also have a substantial effect. Your goal should be to monitor all current and potential forces in the marketplace.

Continuous monitoring was a luxury in the 1970s. In the 1990s it will be a necessity because ongoing strategic decisions require a continuous stream of information.

The purpose of this book is to promote the concept of business intelligence, to provide a framework for implementing an intelligence function and to offer the benefit of my experience in industry so that you can avoid the pitfalls along the way.

Chapter 1

The Need for Business Intelligence

A sharp rise in company intelligence activities has occurred in the last few years. Why is this so?

Companies are now realizing that timely and relevant information about competitors, customers and suppliers is necessary for making good strategic business decisions. Companies now know that a "once-a-year" analysis of their business environment is not enough.

Business intelligence has evolved as a hybrid function of strategic planning and marketing research activities. In the 1970s, companies were just starting to engage in strategic planning activities on a broad scale. Competitor analysis, customer analysis and supplier analysis were important ingredients in that overall process. However, most companies were not organized to collect and analyze the information in a routine and systematic way. In addition, research and planning activities were separate functions, not integrated.

The emphasis in the 1970s was on **developing** strategies. Today's focus is on **implementing** them. Because of the new emphasis, strategic decisions must be made on an ongoing basis. Ongoing strategic decisions require a continuous stream of information. Business intelligence systems provide this continuous stream.

The number of companies developing intelligence groups has risen sharply. It is not uncommon to find the job title of Manager of Competitive Analysis on a company's organization chart. The concept of business intelligence has been around a long time. But, in the 1980s, it has finally come of age.

Business intelligence does not require the knowledge and use of sophisticated techniques or the development of new skills that are not currently available somewhere in most organizations. Rather, it is focusing existing skills and techniques in a direction and for a purpose which is new to many companies. As of this writing, few companies have organized and aggregated their resources effectively to get the job done.

As with many fresh business ideas, general acceptance in the business world is slow. The idea of business intelligence has been slow to evolve but has picked up momentum over the past few years. Your company may no longer have the luxury of waiting to implement a business intelligence function.

Positive Results

You may ask, "Why engage in business intelligence activities?" Perhaps the most important reason is to avoid surprises. Holiday Inn used to advertise "The best surprise is no surprise." This maxim also applies to business intelligence. Nothing is worse than to be surprised by a competitor's move in the marketplace, especially when the information could have easily been obtained well in advance. Business intelligence can help to identify threats and opportunities in the marketplace and it can help companies gain competitive advantage by decreasing the reaction time.

The best way to illustrate the benefits of business intelligence is through examples. The mini case situations outlined below show how companies are using intelligence to gain competitive advantage.

Acquisition of a Major Competitor

Situation: Employees of a large manufacturer had heard rumors of a significant competitor being acquired. The acquisition would provide the competitor with the additional resources it needed to become a national threat by expanding its previously narrow product line and expanding its sales force.

Result: The rumor was confirmed in time for the company to prepare a marketing program to address the market changes.

A Competitor's New Product Strategies

Situation: A medium sized manufacturer of consumer electronics equipment was facing declining sales and market share because of the inroads of two privately held companies. Company management felt these two companies were gaining market share because of new product features being offered.

Result: The competitor's product strategies were determined through interviews with industry sources. The company modified its own product design to avert further market share erosion.

Construction of a New Plant

Situation: A large consumer products manufacturer discovered that a major competitor to several of their product lines was building a new plant. It was unknown whether the plant would produce directly competing products and, if so, what competitive advantage the competitor hoped to gain by constructing the new facility.

Result: Discussions with community leaders, architects, construction personnel and plant management revealed the competitor's plant was slated to produce directly competing products. It was also learned that the new plant was being designed to significantly reduce manufacturing costs. It appeared that the competitor would begin competing on the basis of price rather than differentiation. As a result, the company modified its sales approach to deflect the price issue and build on the strength of their product features.

Development of a Revolutionary New Product

Situation: A health care equipment provider was interested in knowing the research and development projects of a key competitor.

Result: The competitor was found to have several new products under development. One of these products had the potential of significantly altering a key part of the industry. As a result, the company redirected the priorities of its R & D group.

Business Intelligence has many positive results for organizations, large and small, in almost every industry. Company size and market served are not limitations to collecting intelligence.

What Is Business Intelligence?

Business intelligence is comprised of many different types of information:

- Competitor Intelligence

- Market Intelligence

- Product Intelligence

- Customer Intelligence

- Technological Intelligence

- Environmental Intelligence

Business intelligence is an analytical process that transforms raw data into relevant, accurate and useable strategic knowledge. It is information about a competitor's position, performance, capabilities and intentions. It is information about the driving forces within the marketplace. It is information about specific products and technology. Finally, it is information external to the marketplace such as economic, regulatory, political and demographic influences.

Continuous monitoring of competitors, customers, suppliers and other industry forces should be an integral part of the overall strategic management function of companies. This is illustrated in Figure 1-1. Continuous monitoring prevents a company from being surprised. By keeping apprised of industry developments and competitive activities, a company can take appropriate and timely strategic action.

Figure 1-1
Business Intelligence Function

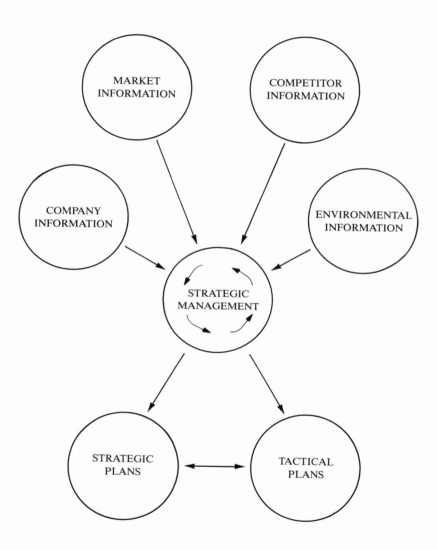

Organizational Impact

The business intelligence function has evolved slowly within most organizations. A review of the intelligence function in hundreds of companies suggests that there are four stages in the evolution.

Stage 1 companies have no particular strategic management or business intelligence capabilities.

Stage 2 companies have a half-time person, a full-time person or perhaps two full-time people assigned to gather and analyze intelligence. This usually takes the form of a limited library or research function.

Stage 3 companies represent those that have a business intelligence system in place. They are routinely gathering and analyzing business information. They have established a manual filing system for competitor, product, technological and other intelligence. This information becomes ongoing input for the strategic management function. However, strategic management and business intelligence functions are not yet integrated.

Stage 4 companies are those that have a comprehensive business intelligence system in place and working effectively. These companies have started to develop mechanized data bases and have fine-tuned their overall procedures for gathering and analyzing business intelligence.

The historical problem with business intelligence has been that it has not been organized. It is performed in a random haphazard manner by employees using only the most common sources of information. The employees read trade journals. They attend trade shows. They talk to their salespeople or have them record intelligence on their call reports. But they don't go beyond these kinds of activities to find the most valuable information that is available.

As much as 95 percent of intelligence is available just for the asking. The challenge is to build an informal intelligence organization that actively seeks out the information in a routine and systematic manner. This does not imply a large mechanized system or organizational empire. It means a formalized process for gathering and analyzing information.

Strategically managed companies have many common characteristics. First, they tend to have widespread strategic thinking which reflects and is based upon an intimate knowledge of the business environment. They also have a pragmatic emphasis on strategy implementation as opposed to strategy development. Perhaps most importantly, they have a supportive corporate organization and style. These companies have acknowledged that business intelligence plays an essential role in the overall process of strategic thinking and in the effective implementation of plans.

What this suggests is that the culture of the strategically managed company demands comprehensive, continuous business intelligence as input to the management process at all levels of the organization.

Effective strategic management does not start or stop with senior management. Business intelligence must not either! For example, the sales organization needs to know what the competition is offering and how the company's products and services can be differentiated. Production and distribution managers need to know what new techniques are being used to improve quality, maximize efficiency and reduce costs.

Just as business intelligence is used at all levels it must also be collected at all levels. Intelligence gathering must be done by the CEO down to the lowest clerk on the totem pole. Wherever and whenever business intelligence is found it must be summarized, collected and disseminated to those in the organization who need it. This process must become a natural part of the daily business routine.

Organizing to make business intelligence happen does not require an extensive centralized staff, sophisticated systems and techniques, and a large budget. What it does require is a small number of people and just one coordinator who maximizes time by utilizing others in the organization. The coordinator actively promotes data gathering, summarizes the results, prepares reports and distributes information to those that need it. Others throughout the organization collect data and analyze its potential impact.

The remaining chapters of this book discuss a systematic process for gathering and analyzing intelligence. The intent is to help you develop a business intelligence system quickly and on a cost-effective basis. Most companies are looking for an intelligence system which gives them a maximum amount of intelligence for the least cost. The approach outlined in this book will yield that result.

Chapter 2

Narrowing the Focus for Efficiency

The potential sources of information are limited only by one's imagination. Hundreds of reference works, directories and other indexed material are available for locating published information. Thousands of people are available to direct you to published data or provide non-published information. The objective of this chapter is to guide you toward potential sources to help shortcut your data gathering efforts.

At the beginning of the information gathering process, ask the questions, "Why am I looking?" and " How does this information tie into the company's overall plans?" The answers to these questions establish the focus of your research.

Understand the Market

First, you should begin by identifying who the competition truly is. Most companies feel they already know. However, many companies have inaccurately defined their market and consequently have failed to identify the true competitors.

Though it may be hard to believe, many companies do not know who their competitors are because they have not yet defined what business their own company is in. They are unable to precisely define their competition in different product/market segments. For example, a maker of kitty litter initially defined its business as Feline Waste Treatment and Removal. However, the product was used for many other purposes such as soaking up oil and grease in factories and service stations. Eliminating the word "Feline" redefined the business and opened up scores of additional competitors.

During the process of identifying your competitors, you must view your business from two distinct but related points of view: 1) from a competitor's viewpoint, and 2) from a customer's viewpoint. In the short run these views can differ significantly. In the long run they are the same.

The view from the customer's perspective is always the most important of the two views. Ultimately, the customer's view of the alternative products or services available to meet a given need drive the market and your overall definition of it.

Focus On Key Success Factors

As with almost every business situation, the volume of information requests greatly exceeds your ability to service them. You need to set reasonable objectives for the types of information you collect. These objectives must be set so that the intelligence effort has the greatest impact on the company's ability to generate a competitive advantage.

A company's mission, objectives, goals, strategies and tactics (e.g., the strategic plan) are developed and focused to achieve key success factors. Key success factors describe what a company must do well to succeed in a given industry. Theoretically, significant competitive advantage can be gained by achieving the key success factors. Business intelligence goals and activities should be designed to support the strategic plan and should be focused on achieving the key success factors. The four types of success factors are listed below:

- Environmental

- Enterprise

- Industry Unique

- Company Unique

Environmental success factors generally influence all businesses to some extent. Examples of these success factors might include growth in the GNP, general level of business taxation and the degree of business regulation. Although the level of control your business has over these factors is minimal in many cases, their impact can be substantial. These factors become "key" success factors only when they significantly affect your own company **more** than your competition.

Enterprise success factors are common to all companies. For example, a key enterprise success factor may be to recruit, hire and train the best possible people. Other examples might include general operating efficiency and cost control. The level of control your business has over these factors is high.

Industry unique success factors arise because of the markets that are being served or the unique aspects of the companies in those markets. An example of an industry success factor might be the need to develop a brand name in a consumer market or providing good service in the distribution business.

Company-unique success factors are those that apply to a specific company. They may be factors which are not necessary for other companies to be successful. For example, a company-unique success factor may be to remain a non-union shop or to be the low cost producer in a given market to maintain competitive advantage.

Knowing your key success factors helps to prioritize the "truckloads" of potential information to be collected. For example, suppose your product/market segment had the following rank-ordered key success factors:

1. Fast/Efficient Service

2. Product Quality

3. Product Features

4. Financial Strength/Profitability

5. Image/Brand Name

6. Price

Under this scenario, the most important information to collect and maintain would be information about the services offered by the competition and details about how they deliver each service. Next, product quality information of each competitor's product would be collected, primarily from the customer's perspective but also by performing product comparisons and reverse engineering. Reverse engineering is the process of buying competing products or services and analyzing their components. This analysis would also yield information on the features of the product or service.

Include Direct, Indirect and Potential Market Forces

Although information gathering should be focused, it should also go beyond a review of direct market forces and include indirect and potential forces.

Direct forces include companies with the same or similar customers and suppliers using the same or competing technologies. For example, makers of bar soap compete with makers of bar soap.

Indirect market forces include companies with substitute products or services. For example, aspirin manufacturers compete with the makers of Tylenol. Indirect forces may also be environmental forces such as economic, regulatory and political influences.

Potential market forces include companies not in the market that could be with minimal product or service changes. For example, a manufacturer of pumps for the marine industry could modify its design to provide pumps to the oil exploration industry.

Primary emphasis should be put on the **direct** forces. Within this category however, the scope of coverage can be narrowed. The research emphasis should be placed on the dynamics which have a maximum impact on the market. In most served markets this represents a relatively small number of forces. They should receive the lion's share of the business intelligence effort on a monthly basis. However routine scanning of **indirect** and **potential** forces should also be performed at least quarterly.

To summarize, you should use the rank of the key success factors to prioritize the alternative types of intelligence you might collect. The key success factors link your intelligence gathering activities to what is important in the market from a competitive standpoint. Next, you should focus on direct market forces. By using this approach you can determine the 20% of available information that yields 80% of the intelligence value. Again, the overall objective of any business intelligence function should be to gather the most meaningful and relevant information at the least possible cost.

Chapter 3

Gathering Published Information

Gathering published information is the most widely employed business intelligence technique. Literally millions of sources can provide potential intelligence "tidbits". Your objective, however, is not to collect millions of items but to collect only those items which are necessary. Chapter 2 described how to narrow the focus of information gathering and how to determine what is most important to collect. This chapter gives direction in identifying potential published sources and describes the "how-to's" of data collection.

Consult With Librarian and Legal Counsel

The company's librarian and legal counsel are without question the best places to begin the search for published information. Librarians can be very helpful in short-cutting the overall search for sources of information. They are trained in information sources and are usually naturally curious people who greatly enjoy assisting in finding information. They usually have at their disposal, or have access to, directories, indexes and other relevant materials. If they don't have direct access to the information, they frequently know where to find it.

Legal counsel can also be helpful in the search for information. They are especially knowledgeable in government filings and documents which may be obtained through the Freedom of Information Act. They may also know about current legal proceedings of companies in the industry and the type of information made public during those proceedings.

The 25 Best Sources of Published Information

The sources in Exhibit 3-1 represent the 25 best places to start when looking for published information. All are available at public libraries or from external data bases. Exploiting these 25 sources usually yields a wide variety of information on almost any company in the world. Further reference information on these sources is shown in Appendix L.

Exhibit 3-1

25 Best Places to Start

■ **Directory of On-line Data Bases**
—An alphabetical listing of available on-line data base services and the type of information contained in each data base.

■ **Where to Find Business Information**
—A list of over 5000 publications, by subject matter, that are published in English.

■ **Encyclopedia of Associations, 19th Edition**
—A descriptive listing of over 20,000 trade, professional, labor, and fraternal associations and societies.

■ **Million Dollar Directory**
—Contains address, names of key management personnel, approximate sales figures and names of divisions for United States Companies.

■ **Thomas Register of American Manufacturers**
—An alphabetical listing of over 120,000 manufacturing firms and the products they manufacture.

■ **Business Information Sources**
—A biblography of business information sources of a wide variety of topics including economic trends.

■ **Business Periodicals Index**
—An index, arranged by subject matter, of articles published in the most important business journals.

■ **Directory of Directories**
—Details the type of information covered, the frequency of publication and the price of over 7,800 business and industrial directories.

Exhibit 3-1, Continued

25 Best Places to Start

■ **Dun and Bradstreet's Principal International Businesses**
—A directory of descriptive and sales information for 70,000 companies in over 100 countries.

■ **Encyclopedia of Business Information Sources**
—Lists books, periodicals and other sources of information for over 1,200 business topics.

■ **Guide to American Directories**
—Contains information about 8,000 professional and trade directories of United States organizations and companies.

■ **Moody's Investors Service: Moody's Manuals**
—A total of seven manuals containing descriptive and financial information for companies in various industry groups.

■ **Standard and Poor's Register of Corporations, Directors, and Executives, United States and Canada**
—Lists addresses, names and brief background information on key management personnel, and sales information for approximately 45,000 corporations.

■ **Ulrich's International Periodicals Directory**
—A listing, by subject matter, of over 62,000 international periodicals.

■ **Value Line Investment Survey**
—Weekly reports of 1,700 stocks in 80 industries.

■ **Ward's Directory of 51,000 Largest U.S. Corporations**
—A listing, by sales size, of the largest corporations in 21 manufacturing and 37 non-manufacturing standard industrial classification categories.

■ **World Directory of Multinational Enterprises**
—Lists product profit and sales information, merger histories and subsidiary locations for multinational enterprises.

Exhibit 3-1, Continued

25 Best Places to Start

■ **Directory of Wall Street Research**
—Lists companies that are researched by security analysts. Provides company information as well as information on brokerage and research firms and research reports.

■ **The Top 1,500 Private Companies**
—Lists the largest private companies in the United States and provides descriptive and sales information for each company listed.

■ **Predicasts F & S Index United States**
—An index of articles about United States companies and industries from over 750 newspapers, trade journals and financial publications.

■ **Directory of U.S. Corporations**
—A rank-order listing of the 500 largest U.S. Industrial Corporations, the 500 largest service companies and the 50 leading exporters.

■ **Directory of Corporate Affiliations**
—A listing of 4,500 present corporations and their domestic and foreign divisions.

■ **America's Corporate Families–The Billion Dollar Directory**
—A listing of 8,500 parent companies with more than $50 million in sales and their subsidiaries and divisions.

■ **Europe's 10,000 Largest Companies**
—A listing of the largest industrial, transport and trading companies in Europe.

■ **Dun's Business Rankings**
—A rank-order listing of over 7,500 United States companies and their address, sales volume and key management personnel.

Order Materials Requiring Longer Lead Times To Obtain

Many published sources are difficult to find and time consuming to obtain. Therefore, longer lead-time materials should be ordered as quickly as possible.

Typical long lead-time materials include annual reports, product literature and credit reports on the companies to be analyzed. In addition, requests for any available information from federal, state and local sources may take months to receive. There may also be a variety of materials available through trade associations or other industry sources which should be ordered in advance.

The Value of Clipping Services

Clipping services are an excellent way to gather information on companies or subjects on an ongoing basis. Clipping services usually clip articles from newspapers, magazines, trade journals, press releases and other regularly published sources. A few clipping services provide worldwide coverage. Their coverage in the United States and Canada is virtually 100% of all newspapers, magazines and trade journals. In other parts of the world, the coverage is as high as 80% to 90%.

Clipping can be done on a company name, a division name, a product name or on some other subject (e.g. insecticides, AIDS, etc.). Typical prices are $30 per month per company or subject plus 70 cents per clipping. These prices relate to clippings from U.S. publications. Clipping from non-U.S. publications usually averages around $60 per company per month.

In the case of international clipping, translation becomes a problem. Translation firms should be engaged to translate headlines and summary information only. To keep the cost down, the full text of international articles should be translated only when the headlines and summaries indicate that the article may yield valuable intelligence. Translation costs can average from $300 to $600 per month.

Why clipping? Clipping is much less expensive than individual subscriptions. When you begin to add up the cost of all of the newspapers, magazines and trade journals plus the cost of clerical personnel reading and clipping the articles on an ongoing basis, clipping by a third party becomes a much more attractive alternative.

Clipping also provides very comprehensive coverage. It covers local newspapers in small towns where competitor operations are located. Some of the best intelligence is located in local newspapers. What may warrant a paragraph or nothing at all in *The Wall Street Journal* may be front-page news in the local newspaper. Typically, these stories include interviews with general managers, CEO's or other key personnel who tend to provide much detail on future plans and strategies of the company.

Clipping services also provide functional as well as industry coverage. For example, they clip articles in periodicals such as Administrative Management, Mechanical Engineering or Industrial Design. Publications such as these are less frequently subscribed to but they sometimes yield very good intelligence. The articles usually include interviews with company personnel who are not aware of the rules regarding disclosure of company information.

Two of the best clipping sources are listed below. Both provide worldwide coverage:

■ Bacon's Clipping Bureau, 332 South Michigan Avenue, Chicago, Illinois 60604, (312) 922-2400

■ Burrell's Press Clipping Service, 75 East Northfield Road, Livingstone, New Jersey 07039, (201) 992-6600

Annual Report and Other Financial Information

Excellent financial information can be obtained from:

■ Annual/Quarterly Reports

■ Securities and Exchange Commission (SEC) Reports

Annual and quarterly reports can be obtained simply by calling the company of interest and asking for the report. Obviously, this works well for public companies and not so well for privately held companies that may not want to disclose financial information to the public.

Annual and quarterly reports are of value for the financial information they provide if the company is a single product/market company. In other words, large publicly held companies tend to have many business lines but your company might only compete with one line. Traditionally, these large corporations blend the financial results of all of their lines so that any one business line cannot be distinguished. Other intelligence sources may be necessary to obtain the financial information you seek.

If SEC information is potentially helpful to you, it is readily available. The reports that are most useful for intelligence purposes are outlined in Exhibit 3-2.

Exhibit 3-2

SEC Reports

10-K: Annual report filed by companies having more than 500 stockholders and $1 million in assets.

19-K: Reports by foreign countries issuing securities in the United States.

10-Q: Quarterly reports filed by the 10-K companies.

8-K: Information about important current developments including change of ownership; acquisitions and dispositions; and bankruptcy and receivership.

F-10: Used by firms during their first two years as a public company. Form F-10 is a combined registration and annual report.

8-A: Used by 1934 Act registrants who plan to issue additional stock.

8-B: Used by companies who have changed their names to notify the stockholders that the company is trading under a new name.

N-1R: Annual report of registered management investment companies.

N-1Q: Quarterly report of registered management investment companies.

To obtain SEC information more quickly, it is possible to contact regional SEC offices directly. The following offices are open to the public and provide current SEC information:

Chicago: 219 South Dearborn Street
Chicago, Illinois 60604 (312) 353-7390

Los Angeles: 5757 Wilshire Boulevard, Suite 500 East
Los Angeles, California 90036 (213) 468-3098

New York: 26 Federal Plaza, Room 1100
New York, New York 10007 (212) 264-1615

Washington: 450 Fifth Street, NW
Washington, DC 20549 (202) 272-7450

Information can also be obtained directly from Disclosure, Inc. Disclosure provides SEC information in an electronically readable format. Their address is:

Disclosure, Inc.
5161 River Road
Bethesda, Maryland 20816 (800) 638-8241.

Some large metropolitan and university libraries have financial information on hand through Disclosure or other sources.

Additional sources of financial information are illustrated in Exhibit 3-3.

Exhibit 3-3

Other Sources of Financial Information

Sales:	– D & B or TRW credit reports
Labor and Fringe Benefits	– Union contracts – Local wage surveys
Raw Materials:	– Supplier brochures and price lists
Equipment:	– Supplier brochures
R & D:	– Trade association reports
Buildings:	– Chamber of Commerce literature – Local development commission literature

Federal Sources of Information

A great deal of information is available from the federal government. This source is not recommended as a primary source, but as a supplement for certain bits and pieces of information that may be helpful in the overall intelligence process. The best approach is a three-step process for attacking federal sources. Begin by contacting the sources listed in Exhibit 3-4.

Contacting this group of federal sources generates many additional sources. The next group of federal sources may provide needed statistics related to international trade, labor and productivity. These sources are listed in Exhibit 3-5.

Hopefully, your initial contacts within the federal government generate additional sources of information relevant to your search. The objective is to network your way through the federal government in an attempt to find the information. The Library of Congress alone has over 80 million items of information. Clearly, a large amount of information is available. However, you may be disappointed when little is relevant to your particular intelligence need.

You might try obtaining information from various governmental agencies by submitting a request under the Freedom of Information Act, but this is usually a slow process and may yield very little detailed information. Many times you request information through the Freedom of Information Act which was originally given to the government with the stipulation that it be labeled confidential or proprietary. In these cases, the government forwards your request to the company in question and allows them to identify or edit the information that is not to be released.

Exhibit 3-4

Federal Sources - Step #1

■ U.S. Department of Commerce Library
(202) 377-2161 Reference Services

■ Bureau of Industrial Economics
U.S. Department of Commerce
(202) 377-4356 100 Industry/Company Analysts

■ Information Central
American Society of Association Executives
(202) 626-2742 Information on Associations

■ National Referral Center
Library of Congress
(202) 287-5670

■ Office of Legislative Information
U.S. House of Representatives
(202) 225-1772 Legislation and Pending Bills

■ Congressional Research Service
(202) 224-3121 Industry/Subject Information
(available through your Congressmen only)

Exhibit 3-5

Federal Sources – Step #2

- Bureau of Economic Analysis
  U.S. Department of Commerce
  (202) 523-0777 National, Regional,
  International Statistics

- Foreign Trade Reference Room
  U.S. Department of Commerce
  (202) 377-2185 U.S. Import and Export
  Statistics

- World Trade Statistics
  U.S. Department of Commerce
  (202) 377-4855 World Import and Export
  Statistics

- Bureau of Labor Statistics
  U.S. Department of Labor
  (202) 523-1239 Labor and Productivity
  Statistics

State Governmental Sources of Information

Many kinds of information may be obtained from state government sources. Examples include the following:

- Directories of companies

- Articles of incorporation

- Financial information on regulated firms

- Government contracts

- Prospectuses

- Environmental impact studies

- Uniform commercial code filings

- Occupational safety and health information

- License information

- Labor information

- Franchise information

- Consumer protection information

Information available from state sources varies by state. It is usually best to start with the state information operator or the Governor's office. Directories of state information may also be available.

Local Information

Local information can yield very detailed and specific information about a company's local operations.

Local information includes:

- Real estate deeds and property records

- Maps, aerial photographs, surveys

- Building permits

- Complaints about firms or products

- Health inspection information

Real estate deeds and property records can yield much information. They contain a description of the property which usually includes the overall size of the property and a brief description of the buildings. The deeds may also contain the purchase price of the property and tax assessment information. Tax assessment information can be useful in providing an estimate of the market value of the property.

In many areas it is illegal to fly over a facility for the purpose of taking aerial photographs. Quite often this isn't necessary. Many local governmental bodies already have aerial shots, and copies can be obtained for a small fee. These photographs have obvious uses, but be sure to check the date the picture was taken; it may not be current.

Building permits and the information provided to obtain them describe new facilities or improvements to existing facilities. In many cases the cost of the building permit can be used as a guide to the value of the construction.

Health inspection information can be used to gain general information regarding the operating conditions inside the facility. It may also yield the number of employees at a given location.

Local sources of information are listed in Exhibit 3-6.

Exhibit 3-6

Local Government Sources

- County or City Clerk

- Recorder or Register of Deeds

- Property Appraiser or Tax Assessor

- Planning Department

- Building Department

- Consumer Protection Agency

- Health Department

Conduct Data Base Searches

External data bases can be extremely useful in finding company information related to events of today or events in the past. Data bases virtually eliminate trips to the library. Many of the reference books that once required manual searching are now available on-line through a computer terminal. For example, in one four-hour on-line search session, one can gather the same amount of information as might take four weeks of manual library research. This makes data base searching much less costly than manual data gathering.

Are data bases difficult to use? No! A person can become fully productive after one-half to one day's training. Thousands of data bases are available through "supermarket" data base vendors. The favorite supermarkets are Dialog, Nexis and Newsnet.

Dialog contains more than 55 million records which provide references to technical reports, newspapers, journals and magazine articles and statistical data. The data bases in Dialog are regularly updated to provide the most current information available. Dialog allows a user to obtain information as specific or as broad as desired.

Nexis is an on-line, full-text data base of news and business information. It contains information from over 150 major publications and news services.

Newsnet contains 300 services from independent, authoritive publishers representing dozens of industries and interest areas. Newsnet allows a user to read an entire newsletter or just scan headings.

The various individual data bases contained in these supermarkets are listed in Appendix E.

Many kinds of intelligence can be gathered from on-line searches, including:

- Sales, size, financial statement information

- Future strategies

- R & D activities

- New product developments

- Trademark and patent information

- Forecasts

- Market research findings

Some of the best data bases available through the supermarkets are listed in Exhibit 3-7.

Exhibit 3-7

The Best External Data Bases

■ **Dun & Bradstreet**
—contains addresses, financial and marketing information on 2,000,000 U.S. business establishments. International Dun's Market Identifiers contains directory listings, sales volume, marketing data and references to parent companies in over 130 countries. The Million Dollar directory contains addresses and financial and marketing information on over 110,000 companies.

■ **Electronic Yellow Pages**
—contains directory listings by Standard Industrial Classification, (SEC) codes.

■ **Thomas Register**
—contains lists of products and manufacturers. This publication covers 123,000 U.S. companies, both public and private, which supply over 50,000 types of products and represent over 102,000 brand names.

■ **Trinet**
—provides sales, financial and marketing information on U.S. establishments with 20 or more employees. This is an excellent source for private companies or small business units of large companies.

■ **Disclosure**
—provides SEC information for approximately 9,000 publically owned companies.

■ **Standard & Poors**
—provides news coverage and financial reports on more than 10,000 publically held corporations.

■ **Moody's**

—provides descriptive and financial information for companies on the New York and American stock exchanges, plus 13,000 of the most active companies traded over the counter. This publication also provides financial and business information on 13,000 publically held U.S. corporations and 3,900 international corporations.

■ **Investext**

—provides the full text of industry and company research reports generated by financial analysts from leading investment banking firms in the U.S., Canada, Europe and Japan.

■ **Predicasts**

—offers 10 data bases which provide business news line of business information from annual reports, new product information and abstracts of published forecasts for several industries in the U.S. and internationally.

■ **Derwent**

—provides patent information from 7,000,000 patent documents, giving details of over 3,000,000 inventions.

■ **Who's Who**

—contains biographical information on accomplished men and women of the U.S., Canada and Mexico.

All of the data bases listed in Exhibit 3-7 are accessible in one search session on Dialog.

The only requirements for conducting on-line searches are a telephone and a computer or terminal which has a modem and printer. Almost any computer terminal or communicating word processor can access external data bases. Supermarket data base vendors provide training at little or no cost.

The charges and the basis for charging vary by supermarket. Charges are based on connect time and the number of records retrieved and/or printed. The supermarkets tend to have lower rates for off-peak hours. The total cost for a comprehensive search on one company in three supermarkets ranges from $300 to $1,000 (or an average of $300 to $500) per company.

It is not important to know the names of specific data bases that are available such as Trinet or Derwent. It is only important that you know the types of information that you want to obtain.

For example, you may want to obtain sales and marketing information about the XYZ Company, a chemical concern. You are particularly interested in any new products they may have developed after January 1, 1986. In a typical data base search using the Nexis supermarket, your search logic might be (XYZ COMPANY) AND (MARKETING) AND (NEW PRODUCTS) AND DATE AFT 1/1/86.

This is a simplified example. In some data bases, you might have to state that XYZ is a chemical company and that your primary interest is to obtain articles as opposed to reference material. The general search logic forms the basis for the on-line search session.

Data bases are excellent for finding historical information. Continuous monitoring of companies from today forward is best accomplished by the use of clipping services. The clipping services minimize the need for ongoing data base searches for articles. However, you should probably continue data base searches for reference information as your needs dictate.

Other Sources

Your search for published information never comes to an end. For the newcomers to business intelligence (organizations in health care, telecommunications, banking and insurance), additional industry-specific sources of published information are listed in Appendices A, B, C and D.

You can see that gathering information from published sources can be a time consuming activity. It is no wonder that companies in general devote too much of their attention to published sources and ignore the more important non-published sources.

Many companies use an information workshop to identify information needs and sources. The information workshop is an informal exchange between representatives from each functional area of the company. Participants in the workshop are required to submit a list of their information needs and current sources. Consolidation of these lists by the workshop facilitator usually reveals the company is missing only a few items of information. In other words, most of the information already exists somewhere in the organization, either in published or non-published form.

Non-published sources exist both within and outside your company. They consist of knowledgeable people in the industry who are willing to share information if asked. Chapter 4 describes the "how-to's" of uncovering the buried treasure inside your own organization. Chapter 5 discusses specific techniques for gathering non-published information from external sources.

Chapter 4

Gathering Non-Published Information from Internal Sources

This chapter looks at the various functional areas of an organization and highlights information that may exist within each area. The chapter begins with the most obvious sources of information and moves toward, perhaps, the least obvious. An approach for obtaining this information on a routine basis is then discussed.

Frequently the best intelligence is located right in your own back yard. Most of what you might want to know about competitors, customers, suppliers and the marketplace is probably common knowledge to someone inside your organization. The task is to develop an internal network to extract this readily available information.

Marketing and Sales

Marketing and sales people usually possess a vast amount of industry knowledge. For the most part, they are in the trenches and on the front lines, face-to-face with customers and competitors. At a minimum, they should be able to supply you with competitor or customer information on the following topics:

- Number of sales and marketing employees

- Sales practices

- Distribution channels

- Training programs

- Compensation methods

- Product differentiation

- Pricing practices and trends

- Promotion mix

- Market and customer development programs

- Specific future strategies

A large mattress manufacturer wanted to obtain information on their competitors. It was suggested to the president that a survey be developed and administered to the marketing and sales people at the various plants.

The president seemed reluctant to take this approach because he maintained that the regional people were not particularly knowledgeable of the competitive situation. Persuasion won out and the president agreed.

The sales and marketing people at each of the plants were interviewed. They provided answers to many questions: competing products, product mix, customer mix, top ten customers, and geographical coverage, to name a few. When all of this information was correlated, no further research was needed.

In another engagement, a major publishing company requested a review of its competitor intelligence system to improve the level of information provided. Interviews were conducted with people at all levels throughout the organization. Because salespeople usually have a wealth of information, one hour was allotted for each interview.

In one instance, the interview exceeded four hours. The salesperson knew absolutely everything about every competitor and customer. Among other things, he knew the locations of all of the competing plants, their product sales volume, the characteristics of the machinery in the plant, how many shifts were running, and the number of people per shift. When asked "Why haven't you ever told anyone what you know?", he responded, "Nobody ever asked!"

When questioned about the comprehensive sales call reporting system that the company had in place, he replied, "In the beginning I was very diligent about filling out my call reports. I filled in customer and competitive information in great detail. However, I never saw what happened to the information that I submitted. I then started to write less and less, and now I am down to a 'one liner' on each report. Nobody questioned this so I assume this is what management requires."

Operations

Operations people can also provide good intelligence. They can tell you more than you might imagine about competitors, customers, suppliers and the overall state of technology within the industry. Their particular areas of expertise are:

■ Nature of processes

■ Facilities

■ Employee mix

■ Cost trends

■ Productivity

■ Status of mechanization/automation

■ Capacity utilization

At the mattress manufacturing facilities, a data collection document was administered to operations people as well as sales and marketing people. The operations people knew virtually everything there was to know about the competitor's organization. In many cases, the plant people played on the same softball league or bowled on the same bowling league as their competitors. Consequently, they were able to regularly obtain competitive information.

The operations people knew the plant locations, the plant output, the products produced, the amount of machinery, the type and quality of machinery, the percentage of capacity being utilized within the plant and many other valuable pieces of information.

Another client situation was a major metropolitan newspaper that requested assistance in developing their strategic plan. During the course of the planning project, a competing paper announced they were going to build a new offset printing plant requiring a significant capital expenditure. The client was very concerned that they might lose substantial market share to the competing paper because the competitor's paper would have a better asthetic appearance.

Management was advised to consult with the operations people. The publisher did not think highly of this idea, but agreed to talk with them. When the problem was posed to the operations people they replied "no problem!" They suggested that a new inking process could be installed at 10% of the cost of the offset presses and would achieve the same kind of offset quality. Clearly, in this instance, the operations people had a key input into the strategic direction of this newspaper.

Accounting and Finance

Accounting and financial people often can provide valuable intelligence. They regularly read the annual reports and other financial information provided by competitors, customers and suppliers.

A major manufacturer of sporting goods asked for assistance in assessing their competition. The president was asked if anyone in the organization had ever plotted the sales of the competing product lines. He did not think that anyone had. In addition, he was asked if anyone had drawn any kind of correlation between a market basket of leading economic indicators and the sales of various kinds of sporting equipment. Again, he didn't think that information was available.

The suggestion was made to talk to the accounting and financial people of the organization. He muttered, "debits, credits, accounts payable, accounts receivable...." In other words, he did not have much faith that accounting and financial people would have the needed information. Against his wishes these people were approached. The chief financial officer was asked if this information had ever been obtained and analyzed. His eyes lit up, he went over to his filing cabinet and retrieved pages and pages of yellow columnar worksheets. The pages were laid out on the table and discussion began about what he had analyzed.

He said, "Yes, we have plotted the sales of the competing products, and we have also drawn a correlation between a market basket of leading economic indicators and the sales of various kinds of sporting equipment. Look what this tells us," he said. "It appears that when the market basket of leading economic indicators started trending downward, the competitors were doing two things. In the short-term they were cutting back on their inventories. It also appears they were making long term product decisions. Instead of introducing three new sets of golf clubs, they introduced two. Instead of introducing four new racquetball racquets, they introduced three." The CFO then offered the punch line, "Our company didn't make these strategic and tactical decisions at that time, and you can see the result by comparing **our** 'bottom line' to **theirs**!".

The president was very upset and asked the CFO, " Why didn't you ever tell us this information was available?" The CFO responded, "Nobody ever asked!"

Engineering

Engineering people can also be very helpful in the overall intelligence effort. Their knowledge lies in:

■ Technology

■ Product development

■ Patents

■ Production process innovation

It was suggested to our mattress client that they engage in a process of reverse engineering (buying the competing products, tearing them apart and analyzing how their products differ from your products). The mattress company was not particularly interested in going through this exercise.

However, all of the competing products were purchased and brought to the engineering department. An interesting scenario then unfolded. All of the mattresses were torn apart and examined in great detail. Cost analyses were prepared based on their own costing system. The result: they discovered a surprising fact. They determined that they could put 20% less material into their mattresses and still have a better quality product than the competition. This 20% dropped right to the bottom line in terms of profits.

Human Resources

Human resources people should not be forgotten in the overall process of business intelligence. One observation that has been made over the years is that human resources people have proportionately more bookshelf space than others in the organization. They have, among other things, competitor and customer recruiting manuals, personnel manuals, training manuals and union contracts.

The chairman of a large railroad wanted to obtain a copy of a union contract of a competing railroad that was signed the prior week. It was suggested that it was not necessary to have a third party obtain it since their human resources people probably had a copy. When the human resources director was approached, not only did this person have a copy of the contract, but it was obtained one hour after it was signed.

These examples illustrate that communication is vital. A mechanism must be developed so that employees can easily communicate competitive and customer information to a central coordinating point. A variety of methods can be used. Companies use a variety of forms and schedules but most find them an unsuccessful medium. Other preferable approaches include:

■ Inbound 800 watts lines.

■ Electronic mail

■ Portable desk-top or hand-held computers

These approaches make it easy for employees to communicate their intelligence "tidbit."

The best approach is to use whatever communication vehicle is the most accepted by the employee. If they regularly use the telephone, use the telephone. If they regularly communicate through a computer, use the computer. Don't develop a complicated set of forms and schedules that have to be filled out manually and sent in to a central point. This approach seldom works.

Some companies have suggested that a financial reward be given to motivate people to provide intelligence. However, this approach is very difficult to administer. For example, a company might pay $10 for each competitive "tidbit". One salesperson may turn in 200 competitive "tidbits" during a given month. An associate may only turn in one. The associate's one "tidbit" may be worth more than the other person's 200 "tidbits" combined. Experience has proven a financial reward system to be less than satisfactory due to the varying degrees of substance attached to each piece of information received.

The best way to motivate people is to make them part of the overall intelligence process. Close the feedback loop and provide them some value-added information in return for what they provide. This feedback loop could be as simple as a monthly news bulletin listing each person's intelligence during the month with their name included as the source.

Employees are motivated when they feel part of the team and their efforts are recognized. When applied toward business intelligence activities, a continuous stream of quality intelligence is usually the result. However, even highly motivated employees need prompting. This requires an active approach by planning and marketing people to prompt employees for intelligence.

Unfortunately most planning and marketing people are passive individuals when it comes to information retrieval. They prefer to rely on published quantitative information, and they prefer to rely on information coming to them rather than digging for it. The key message here is that a passive approach yields very little in the way of intelligence. Eighty percent of what you might want to know about a competitor or about marketplace activities may already be located inside your organization, but it must be actively sought.

The Best Approach

The best approach to gathering internal information can be summarized as follows:

- Develop a "who knows who" list

- Develop an internal network

- Develop monthly call sheets

- Develop information matrices

- Call actively on a monthly basis

It is essential to develop an internal network. Start by creating a "who knows who" list. This list should have the name of every individual you know who could be instrumental in obtaining non-published information from outsiders. An example is shown in Exhibit 4-1.

The next step is to develop a monthly call list. This list should consist of people inside the company that are called by the intelligence coordinator on a monthly basis to determine what is happening in the marketplace. Allocate one to two days each month to **actively** call people on the list and ask them "What's happening with competitor A?; What's happening with competitor B?; What's happening in the marketplace that might have an impact on our strategic and tactical plans?" An example is shown in Exhibit 4- 2.

Ongoing information matrices are also helpful. An example is illustrated in Exhibit 4-3. Trade shows are an excellent place to use a matrix of this kind. People throughout your organization attend trade shows and technical meetings where they have contact with others in the industry. Consider arming them with an information matrix to complete. The traditional approach to trade shows is for attendees to write a one-paragraph memo stating that they attended the show and relating perhaps one competitor "tidbit." Rather than having people writing one-paragraph memos, have them complete a worksheet at the show. This is a very effective approach to gathering a maximum amount of information at no additional cost.

Finally, active calling on a monthly basis will help insure a continuous stream of business intelligence. Appendix F lists key questions that can be asked of various functional people within an organization. This list can be applied both internally and externally. Chapter 5 describes the specific techniques for gathering external non-published information.

Exhibit 4-1

"Who-Knows-Who" List

Personal Contacts			Connections		
Name	Phone/Ext.	Area of Responsibility	Name of Contact	Competitor Company	Area of Responsibility	Link
Tom Smith	314/999-6665 x456	Plant Manager, St. Louis	Fred Connors	Lockwood, Ltd.	Senior Accountant	Bowling League
Linda Abbott	312/666-9999 x780	Human Resources Mgr.	Various	ABC Semiconductor	Personnel Dept.	Former Employees
Charlie Johnson	312/666-9999 x769	V. P. Finance	Ron Smith	Lockwood, Ltd.	V.P. Marketing	Neighbor
Frank Anderson	201/999-5555 x310	Northeast Sales Mgr.	Bill Perry	Ohm Corporation	Product Marketing	Trade Association
Betty Wilson	404/777-8888	Sales Rep. Southeast region	Sam Jones	Electronics, Inc.	Sales Representative	Common Customer
Richard Brown	609/333-4444 x700	Route Mgr./ABC Trucking	Jim Green	Electronics, Inc.	Warehouse Mgr.	Carrier
Harry Benson	312/222-7777 x400	Industry Expert	Joan Long	ABC Semiconductor	Dir. R & D	Consultant
Ann Moore	301/666-1111 x500	Publisher	Various	Various	Semiconductor Technology	Reporter/Editor

Exhibit 4-2
Monthly Call List

Employee	Phone/Extension	Division/Location	Area of Responsibility	Discussion Notes	Date Contacted
Tom Smith	312/666-9999 x243	Specialty Chemicals	Marketing Mgr.	ABC Chemical reduced price of perchlorethelene.	4/1/86
Linda Jones	312/666-9999 x540	Corporate Personnel	Benefits Mgr.	True Chemical Co. reduced employee benefits.	4/2/86
Bob Anderson	314/999-6666 x111	St. Louis	Plant Mgr.	Plant operated at maximum capacity in March. Inventories high.	4/4/86
Frank Wells	201/555-8888	Northeast Region	Salesman	ABC Chemical received large contract for perchlorethelene from Laundry Supply.	4/4/86
Sue Carnes	312/666-9999 x678	Corporate Finance	Sr. Accountant	Overall sales for March up 10%. Perchlorethelene sales down 18%.	4/12/86
Dave Brown	312/666-9999 x876	Corporate R & D	Dir. of Research	Plan to introduce new solvent in June. Lower priced than perchlorethelene.	4/15/86
Sam Johnson	312/666-9999 x456	Engineering	Supervisor	New equipment will reduce production cost of perchlorethelene.	4/16/86
Bill Davis	312/666-9999 x630	Corporate Transportation	Traffic Director	Interstate tarrif rate for chemicals to increase by June 1, 1986.	4/22/86

Exhibit 4-3

Information Matrix

Subject	Capsule Container	Brandt Manufacturing	Smith Corporation	Medical Packaging
Products				
New	None	"Tamper Proof"	Easy Open-Child Proof	None
Dropped	"Safety Seal"	None	Old style-Child Proof	None
Primary Product	"Safe Guard Bottle"	Daily Dispenser	Child proof bottles	Standard Bottle
Weaknesses	Size	Cost	Cap replacement	No safety features
Strengths	Durability	Daily dosage feature	Safety	Cost
Price				
Increases	None	3%—all products	5% "Easy Open"	None
Decreases	25% of Safety Seal bottle	None	None	2% screw on tops
Discounts	5% net 30	Dealer volumes	None	None
Quantity Breaks	1M, 5M,	.5M, 1M, 1M, 2M, 2.5M, 5M	1M, 2.5M, 5M	None
Sales				
Overall Dollars	$5,000,000 per annum	$10,000,000 per annum	Accurate figures	$20,000,000 per annum
Overall Units	200,000,000 per annum	300,000,000 per annum	not available due	800,000,000 per annum
Primary Product Dollars	$2,500,000 per annum	$7,500,000 per annum	to Eversafe acquisition.	$18,000,000 per annum
Primary Product Unit	$30,000,000 per annum	40,000,000 per annum		360,000,000 per annum.
Territory				
Personnel Changes	None	None	None	CEO retired
Geographic Changes	Expanded SW territory	Relocated Newark office	None	None
Primary Geographic Area	New York and vacinity	Southwest	Canada	West Coast

Exhibit 4-3, Continued

Information Matrix

Subject	Capsule Container	Brandt Manufacturing	Smith Corporation	Medical Packaging
Personnel New Hires Layoffs Benefit Changes Compensation Changes	4 New sales people None Offered Dental Ins. 7% increase-Salespeople	2 sales, New York office 10% clerical Employee participation 20% increase, Sr. Managers	None 100 Eversafe employees None Raised commission to 9%	New CEO 75 True Test employees None Salary freeze
Financial Acquisitions Take Over Target Credit Policy Terms and Conditions	None Rumor-Medical Packaging Extending 120 day terms No change	None Rumor-Medical Packaging 15% net 45 Lease labeling Equip.	Eversafe—5/1/86 None Extending 90 day terms None	True Test Pkg. 1/1/86 None 5% net 45 Extended liability claim
Facilities New Plants Plant Closings New Equipment Sale of Equipment New Sales Offices Closing of Sales Offices	Houston, Texas Charlotte, NC Blow molder-Houston, TX All equip.-Charlotte, NC None None	None None None None New York, NY Newark, NJ	3 Eversafe Plants None New Equip. Eversafe Plants All Eversafe Equip. None All Eversafe offices	Boston, MA 3 True Test plants Blow Molder-Boston True Test Equipment Boston, MA 2 True Test offices
Other Relevant Information	Stockholders received extra dividend	None	Litigation-false product claims	Hired Ex-President of Eversafe as CEO

Chapter 5

Gathering Non-Published Information from External Sources

Chapter 3 revealed a wide variety of published data and described where it could be found. Published information provides a good base for your business intelligence system. However, published information is readily accessible by any company in an industry. This fact alone undermines its value as being the "best" intelligence.

Chapter 4 addressed the issue of locating and extracting non-published information from internal sources. Emphasis was placed on the easy availability and value of the information. Chances are, however, that most internal information is shared by more than one employee and is not entirely new intelligence. The information may also be flavored to some extent by the personality of your organization.

Probably the "best" intelligence is obtained from external non-published sources. This intelligence surfaces through discussions with competitors, customers, suppliers or other knowledgeable people in the industry.

59

Gathering information from external sources provides the missing links of information. In many instances this information substantiates or refutes previously obtained data.

The process of interviewing outsiders requires a commitment and must be done actively on a continuous basis. Once you have made the commitment, the task is to determine:

- Who should I talk to?

- What questions should I ask?

- How should I ask the questions?

- When should I classify the information as hard fact versus rumor?

First, you need to begin by expanding your list of external sources. Include all the names of knowledgeable people in the industry that you wish to contact on a regular and ongoing basis.

Intelligence Gathering vs. Basic Marketing Research

Basic marketing research indicates three basic techniques used to conduct interviews:

- In-person interviews

- Mail interviews (surveys)

- Telephone interviews

In-person interviews have many disadvantages. They are seldom spontaneous and often difficult to arrange. In addition, they are the most costly of the three. It is the opinion of some executives that face-to-face interviews are productive in situations where a great amount of information is needed or the subject is complex. However, intelligence gathering usually does not require complex and comprehensive information. In most cases you have already exhausted all published and internal non-published sources and are now down to the bottom line of asking a handful of direct questions.

On the positive side, face-to-face interviews are beneficial when conducted in a social environment such as trade shows or technical meetings. Prearranged in-person interviews do provide a captive interviewee.

Mail interviews (surveys) also have many disadvantages. First, the time requirement to develop an effective, structured questionnaire is enormous. It is very difficult to structure a questionnaire that totally eliminates ambiguity. Secondly, the turnaround time is open ended. Once the surveys are mailed, the interviewer has no control over the response time. Thirdly, you are usually uncertain as to who completes the questionnaire. The task of responding to a survey is often delegated by managers to members of the office staff. Finally, the percentage of response is often very low. However, mail surveys do provide hard-copy responses and are easily tabulated.

Telephone interviewing is perhaps the best method to gather non-published information from external sources. It is quick, flexible and relatively inexpensive. With patience and persistence you can contact a large number of people in a short period of time.

Once a contact has been made you are rewarded with immediate feedback. Armed with your responses, you can quickly determine how much additional information you require. You are also able to determine where and to whom your next call should be made. In the event a new source is identified in a phone conversation, you are able to immediately make contact, referencing the previous phone call. (e.g., "Mr. Smith, I was just speaking with Mr. Davis of the ABC Company and he suggested I contact you....."). Again, it is assumed that when you are gathering information from non-published external sources you are not addressing complex issues and are only in search of a response to three to five pertinent questions.

Telephone Interviewing Can be Learned

Effective telephone interviewing does not require special skills or years of experience. Don't be intimidated by the commonly held belief that you need considerable expertise. If you follow a few simple rules of thumb you arrive at the bottom of the "comfort curve" in a relatively short period of time. These rules of thumb will be discussed in detail, based on the case example in Exhibit 5-1.

Exhibit 5-1

Telephone Interviewing Case Example

A business manager has asked you to find out the status of a new product that has been introduced by a competitor. Specifically, he wants to know when it was introduced and what the sales to date have been. The business manager needs an answer by 5:00 p.m. It is now 3:30 p.m. What should you do?

Step 1: List potential sources of information.

Step 2: Because of the time constraints, rank the sources as first, second or third.

Step 3: Assuming you call the external company directly, list potential people you might call.

Step 4: List the questions to be asked regarding the introduction date and the sales to date.

Step 5: Determine possible objections to your questions.

An example solution for steps one through five is shown in Appendix G. Additional cases are also presented in the appendix.

A good telephone interview requires some up-front homework. This effort is time consuming for the first few calls. However, you should feel confident after a while and should be able to reduce the amount of preparation time.

Let's walk through an example interview related to the case.

Interviewer: "Hello, my name is John Smith and I have an interest in your new product. Can you tell me a little more about it?"

Interviewee: "I'd be very happy to tell you about the product. It is a new product that has been recently introduced which has state-of-the-art technology. You simply take this device, insert it into a chemical solution for 30 seconds, remove from the solution and take a reading based on a scale that has been predetermined."

Interviewer: "Wow, that sounds terrific! I'm surprised that we haven't heard about this new product."

Interviewee: "Well, it was just introduced in August. The national roll-out was in October and we have also signed an agreement with a distributor in the southwest region."

Interviewer: "This is very exciting! I bet this product is doing extremely well in the marketplace!"

Interviewee: "Yes, the product is doing very well. In fact we have made five lots of this product."

Interviewer: "Is that hundreds or thousands?"

Interviewee: "We have sold over a thousand."

Interviewer: "Over a thousand?"

Interviewee: "Yes, we've sold about 1,942."

Interviewer: "These sure must be priced right!"

Interviewee: "Yes, they are. The price ranges from $2.13 to $4.14 depending on the order volume."

This interview depicts some basic but very important interviewing techniques. The interviewer starts out with just a simple statement designed to build initial rapport with the interviewee, "I have an interest in your product."

The interviewer then asks an open-ended question designed to get the person on the other end of the phone talking. Based on this open-ended question, the interviewee starts to describe the details of the product. The interviewer may not have understood all of the details of what the interviewee was talking about, but it did not matter. The interviewer's task was to determine the introduction date and the sales to date of the new product.

Notice the enthusiasm factor after the initial explanation by the interviewee. Enthusiasm is key to gathering information. The more enthusiastic the interviewer is, the more enthusiastic the interviewee is and the greater chance that additional details are volunteered.

Also notice that the interviewer never asks direct questions:

1. When was the product introduced?

2. What have the sales to date been?

The best way to phrase questions is not to phrase them as questions at all. Direct statements work much better than questions in gathering information. Instead of saying, "When was the product introduced?", the interviewer said, "I can't believe that we haven't heard about this product!" This is a direct statement designed to elicit a response. In this case it yielded the introduction date as well as the national roll-out date and information about a distributor agreement.

Notice also the bracketing technique. The interviewer did not have any idea what the sales were but wanted to get into the right ballpark. The question, "Is that hundreds or thousands?" is a bracketing technique. If someone were to ask you what your salary is, you probably would not tell them. However, if they asked you whether you made between $10,000 and $20,000, $20,000 to $30,000, $30,000 to $40,000 or $40,000 and over, you are much more likely to answer that question. The same technique works in gathering intelligence. If you know the range in advance, use the range. If you don't know the range, use the "hundreds or thousands" technique.

The next technique used was a restatement technique. The interviewee said "over a thousand". The interviewer simply restated what the interviewee said. This technique throws the ball back into the court of the interviewee. In this case it generated an exact answer. You may find that you may have to use the bracketing technique and other techniques in series in order to get to the exact answer.

You should also be familiar with a few other techniques. A suggestive or challenging technique works very well when you are trying to gather information that is new or different. For example, you may want to find out who your competitor's joint venture partner is. You have no idea who the joint venture partner might be, but you want a way of eliciting an answer from the interviewee. For example:

Interviewer: "I heard your company is entering into a joint venture with IBM?"

Interviewee: No, it's Burroughs.

This technique works well because people naturally want to correct others. If what you have said is incorrect, most people are quick to tell you the correct answer.

Again, the process of gathering non-published information from external sources requires that you determine the following:

- ■ Who should I talk to?

- ■ What questions should I ask?

- ■ How should I ask the questions?

- ■ When should I classify the information as hard fact versus rumor?

Who Should I Talk To?

Virtually everyone is fair game outside the organization, including labor unions, trade associations, suppliers, distributors, customers and, yes, even competitors!

Labor unions are repositories of much information. For example, they can usually tell you the number of employees at specific facilities, the wage rates, specifics about the current union contracts, perceptions about employee/management relations and the likelihood of strikes. They frequently know the company's hiring plans and the labor skill levels required. This can give you insight into future plans and strategies.

Trade associations provide varying levels of information depending on their relative strength. Many can provide global industry statistics and average member financial information. Using this information you can generate the first draft of a company's financial statements which can be refined using telephone research techniques.

Trade associations also maintain membership directories. These directories are very useful in generating contact names inside the company of interest for use during telephone research. Trade associations are generally not good for providing specific information about a member company unless the member plays a major role in the association's management or operation.

Suppliers can tell you what types of their products, (e.g. parts, raw materials), and what quantities they sell to a specific company. They may also know if they are the specific company's sole source of supply. In many instances a supplier can identify competing suppliers of like or substitute products. This information can be used to help estimate the sales volume of the specific company's end product.

Distributors can tell you how much of your competitors' products they sell. Not only that, distributors frequently carry more than one brand of a given product. They can tell you how the products compare in terms of features, price, quality and serviceability. They can also tell you about your competitor's promotions, such as when they occur and what they offer.

Customers can provide some of the same intelligence as distributors. Salespeople from many companies call on them. Also, customers sometimes belong to "user groups" where customers using the same products on a regular basis meet and discuss, among other things, product usage and problems. This is particularly prevalent in the computer industry.

Competitors can provide you with much information about themselves. Product literature, annual reports and the text of recent management speeches are only a few of the items available. Your best bet, however, is to get non-published information straight from the source.

Just about any organization that does business with the company in question is a potential source of information. For example, joint venture partners frequently know a great deal about their competitors and their capabilities.

Although telephone interviewing can yield much information, you must also be prepared for rejection. Telephone interviewing is a numbers game. You may have to call 10 or 20 people before you find the person that will talk to you. You may then have to call 10 of these people before you find the person who not only talks to you but who also has the answers you are looking for. Because it is a numbers game, be prepared to make hundreds of phone calls to find out relevant intelligence.

The best strategy is as follows:

1. Contact known people first. Contact people that you know within the company of interest, or have your business associates call people they know within the company.

2. Contact lower level employees first:

   ■ 800 numbers

   ■ Customer service

   ■ Librarians

   ■ Senior secretaries

3. Contact the top levels within the organization, such as the general manager or other members of senior management. These people are often willing to talk. Their daily routine includes communicating with securities analysts, employees, community leaders and other outsiders. Senior managers are very verbal people and are very proud of their organization.

Middle managers are difficult. This group of people comprises product managers, marketing managers, planning managers, R&D managers and other similar job functions. Usually, they do not talk. If it is imperative to approach middle management, have the answers which you obtained from lower level employees at hand. Use the middle managers for confirmation only.

A word of caution—Experts are seldom experts!

So-called industry experts (industry consultants, securities analysts, etc.) are seldom experts. These individuals rely on conventional wisdom and are often not in command of current facts. As a result, their opinions and conclusions are often inaccurate. It is advisable to gather information from a variety of sources and confirm the information two or three times before classifying it as a fact versus a rumor.

An example:

> 1945 —
>
> "That damn thing will never go off, and I speak as an expert on explosives."
>
> Admiral Leahy—1945
> From *Men and Atoms*
> by
> William Laurence, 1959

In the example above, Admiral Leahy was the world's foremost authority on explosives. When responding to a telephone interview, he said the atom bomb would never go off. He was wrong! Likewise industry "experts" are frequently wrong.

What Questions Should I Ask?

Almost any question is fair game. However, government regulations dictate that questions related to prices or other terms of sale be omitted. Information to obtain over the telephone can include the following:

- Sales

- Margins

- New products

- Product development

- Process information

- Future plans and strategies

How Should I Ask The Questions?

Guidelines for telephone research can be summarized as follows:

- Be friendly and unassuming.

- Build rapport ("I have an interest").

- Exchange information.

- Ask open ended questions.

- Let the other person do the talking.

- Show great enthusiasm.

When gathering information, consider giving away some information to get some information. In other words, offer a "tidbit" (not necessarily a "hot tidbit") to gain some information. The information that you give away could be something from last week's press release. The information you receive in return is often more valuable.

It is essential that you do some up-front homework. In other words, you need to determine who you are going to call, what questions you are going to ask, in what order you are going to ask the questions and how you are going to ask the questions. In developing your telephone survey instrument you also need to determine every possible objection that the interviewee might have about answering your questions. It is essential that you develop a strategy for overcoming their objections.

Salespeople are experts at overcoming objections. The same techniques they use apply to telephone interviewing. For example, you could ignore an unfavorable question and just charge ahead in an enthusiastic manner. Always ask yourself, "How would a salesperson respond to this objection?"

The information that you give away could be something from last week's press release. The information you receive in return is often more valuable.

Again, specific questions should not be phrased as questions. Statements work much better than questions. Remember to use the five proven techniques:

1. Neutral phrases

2. Suggestive statements

3. Bracketing Techniques

4. Restatement Techniques

5. Challenging Techniques

"Practice makes perfect" in telephone interviewing. Set an

objective to call a competitor once a week for the next month. You should feel very comfortable after the first few calls.

The question then becomes what to do with the information that has been gathered. This is discussed in the next few chapters.

Chapter 6

Guidelines for Analyzing Industry and Market Information

Information by itself has no value until analysis is performed. Analysis puts information in a form suitable for strategic and tactical decision-making.

Many approaches to analysis are in use. This chapter generally describes the traditional approaches and outlines a specific approach for intelligence purposes.

The traditional approaches can be categorized as either micro or macro. The micro approach involves working at a detailed level, utilizing as many statistics as are available. The macro approach is sometimes referred to as "portfolio analysis".

The Traditional Micro Approach

The micro approach to planning is used to build a plan from the bottom up. Generally it is the approach used by people in the organization who develop the strategic and tactical plans for a given product or market. This approach includes a detailed analysis of many market forces, including issues which are beyond the company's control to issues that are totally within the company's control.

Micro analysis necessitates a look at the external environment to determine if factors outside of the company's control might have an impact on the market. This task identifies economic, regulatory, political, demographic and technological factors which could affect the business. As each issue is analyzed, the impact the issue may have on the business is forecasted.

Micro analysis incorporates a review of the markets in which the company compete as well as any potentially served markets. The content of the analysis includes data on market size and growth.

The next step is to examine customers in the served market. The goals are to increase your understanding of major customers and to identify key future changes which might affect the company. The following kinds of questions are asked:

■ What product characteristics are most important: function, quality, price, delivery, or field support? Are these characteristics changing?

■ Are there unfilled customer needs that could be satisfied through product modifications or new product development?

- What is happening in the customer's external environment? How might it affect his or her buying objectives?

- What are the customer's reasons for success or lack of success?

- Is the customer integrating horizontally or vertically?

Micro analysis also includes an examination of competitors. The purpose of this step is to take a close look at the main competing forces in the industry. The goal is for a company to know its competitors as well as it knows itself. As a first step, prepare a list of competitors for each existing or new product line. This list includes competitors making the same type of product or different products which accomplish the same function. Once competitors are listed, they are ranked by size and importance and the major ones are selected for further study. The conclusion of this examination ends with an assessment of key competitor issues.

This task also includes an analysis of technology. Many areas are examined for technological change, including

- Development of processes which make one material more desirable to use than another

- Changes in production technology

- Changes in transportation technology

- Changes in packaging technology

- Obsolescence of products

Finally, company resources and capabilities are reviewed. This review goes much further than just developing a financial analysis, although financial analysis is definitely part of the process. The company's capabilities and weaknesses in each function must be evaluated. For example, the strength of its management team, the capabilities of its data processing, and the manufacturing or operations approach are all evaluated.

The result of the micro analysis is often called a situation analysis. The situation analysis incorporates a summary of the external analysis and the market analysis together with an identification of potential opportunities and threats to the organization. It also includes an assessment of competitive strengths and weaknesses.

The strategic and tactical plans are then developed to use the company's strengths to build on the opportunities identified and to shore up company weaknesses.

The Traditional Macro Approach

In contrast to micro analysis, macro analysis, as part of the strategic planning process, provides a top down perspective. Macro analysis is usually used by central decision makers to outline general strategies for each of their product/market segments and to assist with the overall allocation of company resources.

The traditional macro approach is to utilize portfolio techniques. Essentially, portfolio analysis classifies markets in a two dimensional matrix. One dimension usually reflects some measure of the market attractiveness and the other reflects the company's relative competitive position. Strategy is generally determined by evaluating where your product or service currently is in the matrix and where you would like it to be. The strategy is the means you select to move from your current position to your desired position.

These techniques can also be used to analyze other companies in the industry as well as your own. They are very helpful in reducing the complexity in analyzing a particular company. The most widely used approaches are:

■ The Growth Share Matrix developed by the Boston Consulting Group

■ The Business Screen developed by McKinsey and Co.

■ The Industry Maturity - Competitive Position Matrix developed by Arthur D. Little

The Growth-Share Matrix

The Growth-Share Matrix is probably the most widely used portfolio approach. This matrix is illustrated at a high level here so the reader can get the flavor for the types of analysis that are performed.

The Growth-Share Matrix is illustrated in Figure 6-1. It displays a firm's entire portfolio of businesses by characterizing each individual business unit dollar sales, market share relative to the share of the largest competitor in the industry and the annual inflation adjusted growth rate of the industry in which the unit competes.

The higher a unit's market share, the higher its cash generating ability. This assumption is based on the effect of the "experience curve" and "economies of scale". In other words, a larger firm or a firm with more cumulative production experience should be able to operate at lower unit costs and with better margins than its smaller competitors.

The higher the market growth rate, the higher the unit's cash requirements. Cash input is required to keep pace with a growing market when the strategy is to maintain market share. Additional cash input is required to increase market share. Alternatively, a decrease in share may make cash available.

Market growth slows as an industry approaches maturity. As growth slows, a unit with a large relative market share is able to maintain its market position while generating cash to be reinvested in units that are still growing.

The matrix is separated into four quadrants. Growth is usually classified as "high" or "low" by using an arbitrary cutoff of ten percent. Industries above the cutoff can be thought of as "growing" and those below it as "mature."

Similarly, the cutoff for a "high" and "low" share is usually 1.0; thus a "high" share implies market leadership. The cutoffs can be placed anywhere, the key consideration being that units in the southwest quadrant should be cash generators, those in the northeast should be cash users, and those in the remaining two quadrants should be roughly cash "neutral".

Business units located in each of the four quadrants represent different cash flow characteristics, implying different management strategies. Units in each of the quadrants are typically characterized as follows:

Stars - These business units have high relative market share in high growth industries. Their cash flow position depends on how strong their relative share is and whether cash from operations is sufficient to finance their rapid growth. They may yield positive or negative cash flow or they may be close to cash neutral. As the growth of their industry slows, and if they maintain their share of the market successfully, they start to generate cash to be reinvested elsewhere. As an industry matures, stars move toward the southwest quadrant.

Cash Cows - These business units have dominant relative shares in low growth industries. They typically generate far more cash than they can profitably invest internally. The cash they generate can be used to fund other growing units.

Question Marks - Also referred to as problem children, these units have low relative shares requiring cash input to maintain share in rapidly growing industries. However, because of their low market share, relative to competitors, their cash generating ability is relatively weak. Therefore, they are cash users, and a key corporate strategy question is whether to invest more cash to increase their market share or to phase them out.

Dogs - These are units with low relative market share in slowly growing industries. They may generate enough cash from operations to maintain their own market share, but their profitability is poor and they are unlikely to become significant sources of cash. A possible strategy is to manage these units for cash by allowing share to slide. Because dogs may be modest users of cash with no prospect for future cash generation, they are often referred to as "cash traps".

The Growth-Share Matrix makes many simplifying assumptions and has come under fire in recent years. Nonetheless, it is still a helpful tool in reducing complex situations to a digestible format and thereby aids in the overall analysis.

The Business Screen

The business screen, also referred to as the industry attractiveness - competitive position matrix, is displayed in Figure 6-2.

The vertical axis represents the "industry attractiveness" for each business unit, which is based on a weighted measure of such factors as growth opportunities, strength of competition, regulatory environment or other factors. The measure falls into one of three categories: High, medium and low.

The horizontal axis represents the unit's competitive position in its industry. Competitive position is a weighted measure of such factors as market share, product quality, quality of sales force, among others. The position measure is divided into strong, average and weak categories.

Circles represent individual units. The circle size is proportional to the size of the industry in which the unit competes, while the pie slices represent the market shares of the individual units.

The screen is usually divided into three zones as shown in the figure. The three cells in the upper left corner represent high overall attractiveness. Management would direct investment toward units in this zone. Units plotted in the lower right cells have low overall attractiveness and may be candidates for harvesting or divesting.

Industry Maturity - Competitive Position Matrix

The industry maturity—competitive position matrix, illustrated in Figure 6-3, has characteristics in common with both the growth-share matrix and the business screen. The competitive position for each unit is assessed and plotted in the same way as it is using the business screen approach. However, the vertical axis represents various stages of industry evolution and maturity. In a sense, it is similar to the industry growth axis of the growth-share matrix, where cash cows and dogs are usually seen to be in mature industries, while stars and question marks are in growth industries.

The stages of maturity can be roughly characterized as follows:

Introduction — Rapid growth, rapid changes in technology, emphasis on pursuing new customers, low barriers to entry, changing market shares.

Growth — Growing rapidly, customers beginning to align with producers and fewer new customers, technology spread more widely, market shares stabilizing, higher barriers to entry.

Shakeout — Weaker competitors dropping out, fewer new entries; customers, technology and market shares fairly stable.

Maturity — Customers aligned with producers, stable technology and market shares, high entry costs, broad product lines, very little growth in total market.

Decline — Falling demand, fewer competitors, narrowing product lines.

The steps in this analysis are the same as for both the growth-share and business screen approaches. The difference is that this approach highlights a slightly different aspect of strategy. The primary influence on a unit's strategy is the level of maturity of the industry the unit is in.

Sources of additional information on these approaches are listed in Appendix L.

Figure 6-1

The Growth–Share Matrix

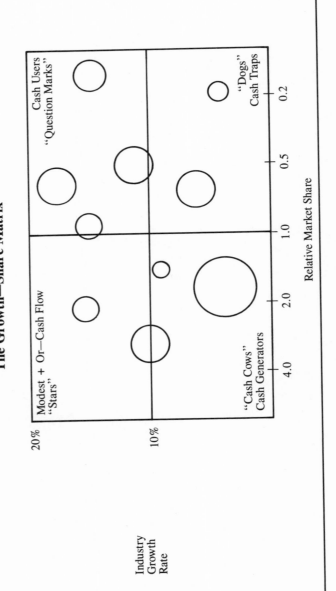

Figure 6-2

The Business Screen

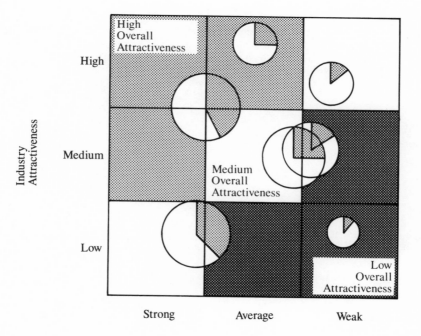

Figure 6-3

The Industry Maturity—
Competitive Position Matrix

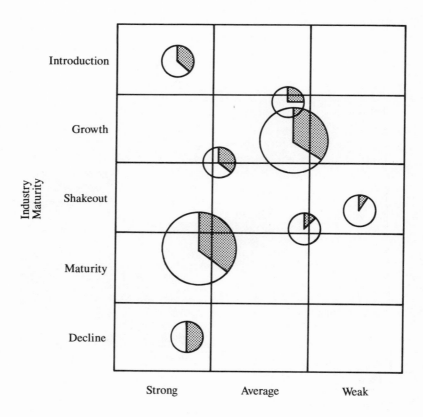

Competitive Position

The Suggested Approach

The micro and macro approaches to analysis can be very detailed and time consuming. They have their weaknesses but generally work well as part of a comprehensive strategic planning process. Business intelligence professionals should have a working knowledge of these approaches. Systematically creating intelligence requires a different approach.

The micro and macro approaches are part of an in-depth analysis which should be performed annually or quarterly as part of a company's strategic plan update. The ongoing analysis of business intelligence requires a simpler approach.

In a business intelligence system, hundreds or thousands of individual pieces of information are obtained. Each piece of information has a place in the intelligence jigsaw puzzle. The task is to quickly determine where the piece fits or, at a minimum, identify the general area where it will fit. Individual pieces may complete a puzzle or start a new one. Over time, the intelligence jigsaw puzzle is completed several times, under different scenarios, and becomes a major input into the analysis process that is part of the strategic plan update.

A coordinator is needed to receive the bits of information and quickly synthesize the information into intelligence. A checklist of key strategic questions will facilitate this activity. These questions should be focused toward customers, competitors, suppliers and other industry forces:

1. Does the information relate to the current strategy of a customer, competitor or supplier?

2. Does the information represent a change in strategy?

3. Does the information reflect long-term changes forthcoming in the market? Product/Service changes? Technological changes? Changes in the structure of the market? Changes in market players?

4. Does the information indicate changes in resources devoted to the market?

5. Does the information describe personality or culture?

6. Does the information suggest changed assumptions about market conditions?

Applying these six questions to each piece of information greatly aids in synthesizing the "truckloads of gathered data" into meaningful and relevant intelligence. Perhaps the last question to be asked is:

Does this piece of information have an immediate impact on your company's future direction? Does it have a **potential** impact?

If the answer to any of the above questions is yes, the information should be categorized and stored. The intent is not to perform a detailed analysis. Rather, it is to systemically identify intelligence that can be used for ongoing management decisions. The intelligence is analyzed in detail at the time of the strategic plan update.

Chapter 7 discusses the "packaging" of the intelligence for various management needs. Chapter 8 will discuss the mechanics of designing an ongoing business intelligence system.

Chapter 7

Synthesizing Information into "Intelligence"

Writing intelligence reports is a most difficult task for company managers. They find it very difficult to synthesize the "truckloads of information" into brief action-oriented reports.

Two problems arise at this point in the intelligence process. First, you have a truckload of information in various stages of completion. Second, senior management has neither the time nor the desire to read a truckload of information. The task at hand is to convert the information you have gathered into succinct "intelligence."

Intelligence gathering is a collective effort and not the effort of one individual. Therefore, pride of authorship should be eliminated. Several other guidelines should be followed when writing intelligence reports. They include the following:

- Identify the essential elements of information.

- Use a bullet-point format.

- Use graphs and charts.

- Avoid the use of numbers.

- State conclusions and supporting information in a concise manner.

- Develop a hierarchical approach.

Identify The Essential Information

A large oil and gas client requested assistance in developing a competitor intelligence system. When they were asked to pull together the information they had on their competitors, they presented a 4,000 square foot room filled with large stacks of competitive material. "This is the information you asked for," they said. "It is everything we have gathered on our competitors over the last 50 years!"

The client was advised to discard everything that was 10 or more years old. It is even doubtful that information which is 10 years old could be considered relevant business intelligence. The client was also advised to extract all pertinent information from the remaining documents and record it on a dictaphone.

Rough rule of thumb..."Probably only 10 important bits of intelligence are found in any stack of material." This approach works well on a "first-time-through" basis.

Use a bullet-point format

How many times have you received a report that is multiple pages and all words? Usually, it sits in your in-basket until you have some spare time...which means you never read it!

Intelligence should be clear and concise. Intelligence should not be a novel. A bullet-point format can convey much information in an easily digestible format.

Use Graphs and Charts

How many times have you received a report that is multiple pages and all numbers? Like the report with all words, it sits in your in-basket.

It takes a few minutes just to figure out the format in which the information is presented. Once the format is digested, it takes more time to extract the important information.

In most instances you can express numerical data with charts and graphs, therefore lists of numbers should be avoided. Graphs and charts can quickly convey important intelligence. Presenting intelligence in a digestible format greatly aids strategic and tactical decision making. It also gains support for the overall intelligence function.

Use a Hierarchical Approach in Reporting

Figure 7-1 illustrates the intelligence hierarchy. It begins at the lowest level with a data base of raw information. From this data base, monthly news bulletins are produced and distributed to individuals within the organization. The next level is represented by competitor profiles which are prepared in either summary or detailed form. The next layer consists of strategic impact worksheets where value starts to be added to the information. It is at this level that intelligence begins to be formed. Even more value is added at the next level which consists of more comprehensive situation analyses. The hierarchy is capped with monthly intelligence briefings and special intelligence briefings targeted toward senior management.

Figure 7-1
Intelligence Hierarchy

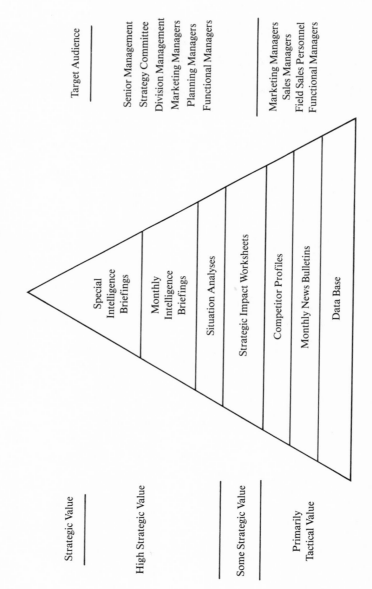

Chances are that you have some of these reports if your company is already conducting intelligence activities. Many companies consider competitor profiles as the primary end result of the information they present. They go no further up the information hierarchy. Competitor profiles are of no strategic value in and of themselves! Before information can have strategic value, analysis must be performed to determine the impact of the information on your organization. In essence, you must move up the hierarchy.

Each layer of the hierarchy is described in Exhibit 7-1.

Exhibit 7-1

Summary of Intelligence Reports

Report Type	Description	Level of Strategic Value	Target Audience	Frequency of Reporting
Monthly News Bulletins	Contains both strategic and tactical information from both internal and external sources.	None	Field Sales Personnel Marketing/Sales Management	Monthly
Competitor Profiles	Contains general information about a competitor, usually maintained in a 3-ring binder. Updates on a continuous basis.	None	Marketing/Sales Management Field Sales Personnel	As required
Strategic Impact Worksheets	Similar to monthly news bulletin but the initial attempt at identifying as items of stragetic/ tactical impact is added.	Low	Marketing/Sales Management Other Functional Managers	Monthly
Monthly Intelligence Briefings	Includes key strategic and news items. Is a bound report. Articles and interview notes are summarized and presented in bullet format for management and included in detail in book.	Medium	Division Management Functional Managers	Monthly or quarterly
Situation Analysis	Summarizes key strategic issues and includes the detailed analyses which supports the summary.	Medium	Division Management Senior Management Functional Managers	As required
Special Intelligence Summary	A one to two page report which identifies an issue, summarizes the key supporting analyses and prepares a recommended course of action.	High	Senior Management	As required

Business Intelligence systems must deal with two types of information about companies: static and dynamic. Static information, by definition, changes infrequently. Company locations, plant sizes and production capabilities are examples of static information.

Static information, once known, need not be reported. Management has neither the time or the inclination to re-read old information. Static information must be stored and used only to assist in the analysis of new dynamic information. Again, competitor profiles, because of the nature of the information they contain, have little or no strategic value.

Conversely, dynamic information changes daily. The reporting needs and the strategic importance of the two types of information differ drastically. Dynamic information describes what is changing about a competitor and is, therefore, information which must be analyzed and reported frequently, preferably monthly.

Dynamic information, taken by itself, may not tell a strategic story. Groups of dynamic information can outline a company's entire strategic plan! This was the focus of discussion in Chapter 5.

As you move up the hierarchy, the dynamic information is sorted by its level of strategic importance. Various analyses are performed so that the impact of the information on the company can be determined.

Exhibits 7-2 through 7-7 at the end of this chapter illustrate each report in the hierarchy.

The data base of raw information is used to generate the monthly news bulletin and to update the competitor profiles where appropriate.

It is on the strategic impact worksheet where strategic value begins to be added. The monthly news bulletin is sorted, summarized, and then an initial pass at determining the strategic or tactical significance of each item is added.

Next, the monthly intelligence briefing combines strategic and tactical information in a bullet format suitable for senior management consumption. This bound report is produced monthly or quarterly and includes detailed articles or interview notes in the back.

Situation analyses and special intelligence briefings are designed to address specific strategic issues which might arise. Of the two reports, the situation analysis contains much more detailed analyses than does the special intelligence briefing. The target audience and purpose of the two reports are the reasons for the difference. Special intelligence briefings are designed for senior management consumption and are only one to two pages long. Situation analysis reports are designed for middle management.

Keys to Successful Reporting

Emphasis should be placed on the following when creating intelligence reports:

- Strategic versus tactical information

- Decision oriented information

- Inclusion of supporting data only if relevant

- Multiple reports versus one large report for levels below senior management

- Distribution to individuals on a need-to-know basis

In Chapter 8 the preparation of these reports in the context of an ongoing intelligence system is discussed.

Exhibit 7-2

Monthly News Bulletins

Monthly news bulletins usually contain both strategic and tactical information. The information is obtained during the month from both internal and external sources. News bulletins are simply listings of information; no value is added. They are used primarily as a tool to promote field input and to communicate across regions. The contents of a news bulletin normally include:

- The information itself
- Information source
- Date the information was received
- An indication of which products, services, markets or functional areas are affected
- Reliability index
  - Rumor
  - Confirmed rumor
  - Fact
  - Hard fact

The users of this report tend to be marketing managers, sales managers and field sales personnel. This report should be prepared monthly in a bullet-point format.

Exhibit 7-2, Continued

Monthly News Bulletins

Example

Date	Competitive Information	Source	Reliability Index
October, 1986	Corporate headquarters has heard a rumor that J.R. Industries has a new plastic bottle in test market. Specifically, the new bottle is a two liter, tamper-proof beverage container that is being test marketed at convenience stores in the Dallas area. In addition, J.R. Industries anticipates introducing the new bottle within 90 days.	Sam Houston (Salesperson)	Confirmed Rumor

Exhibit 7-3

Competitor Profiles

Competitor profiles contain general information about all aspects of the competition, from plant locations to sales and marketing strategies. Information should be collected in a three ring binder that can accommodate basic data and will easily lend itself to the periodic updating of the profiles as new information becomes available. Competitor profiles should be updated on an on-going basis and distributed to marketing managers, sales managers, field sales personnel, and other selected functional managers.

Exhibit 7-3, Continued

Competitor Profiles

Example

Competitor Profile
October, 1986

Company Locations

XYZ Incorporated
Division of ABC International
516 S. East Street
Denver, Colorado

ABC International
11211 Highway B
Calgary, Alberta

Key Management Personnel*

—E. Thompson : Chairman and CEO
—G. Wilder : Vice Chairman and President
—L. Wilson : Vice President of Marketing
—K. Cagney : Vice President and Controller
—C. Donnelley : Vice President of R & D
—M. McCauley : Vice President of Sales

*This section would include background information
on the key management personnel.

Exhibit 7-3, Continued

Competitor Profiles

Plant Locations	Number of Employees	Square Footage
United States: Denver, Colorado	550	320,000
Dallas, Texas	125	75,000
Milwaukee, Wisconsin	350	280,000
Canada: Calgary, Alberta	80	60,000

*This section would include other statistics such as total capacity, capacity utilization, equipment used, etc.

Sales and Sales Trends			Market Share
United States:	$206 million	Growing	38%
Canada:	$98 million	Stable	45%

Exhibit 7-3, Continued

Competitor Profiles

Distribution and Field Sales*

— 23 United States Distributors

— 9 Canadian Distributors

— Western Region Sales: 17 salespeople in three districts
— Midwest Region Sales: 25 salespeople in four districts
— Southern Region Sales: 12 salespeople in three districts
— International Sales: 10 salespeople

Sales Mix

— Retail: 25%
— Institutional: 75%

*This section would include reporting responsibilities, distributor locations, key customer information, etc.

Product Lines

— Mixers
— Slicers
— Blenders

Percent of Sales

36%
49%
15%

Marketing Strategies:

■ Position products as high quality at competitive prices
■ Expand market share by acquiring smaller competitors

Exhibit 7-4

Strategic Impact Worksheet

It is in a strategic impact worksheet that strategic value is added to the information that has been gathered. The worksheet is similar to the monthly news bulletin, but one level of value is added—a "guess" as to the strategic impact or tactical significance of the information. Contents of a strategic impact worksheet include:

- Date and source of information
- Functional impact
- Division affected
- Geographical significance
- Type of information and reliability index

This worksheet format shows qualitative information and the potential strategic impact of each piece of information. It is usually targeted toward marketing managers, sales managers, and other selected functional managers.

Exhibit 7-4, Continued

Strategic Impact Worksheet

Example

Date	Competitive Information	Strategic Impact	Source	Reliability Index
October, 1986	Corporate headquarters has heard a rumor that J.R. Industries has a new plastic bottle in test market. Specifically, the new bottle is a two liter, tamper-proof beverage container that is being test marketed at convenience stores in the Dallas area. In addition, J.R. Industries anticipates introducing the new bottle within 90 days.	J.R. Industries is a new company that has made a large investment into r&d and new product introduction. Because of this, J.R. has been gaining market share rapidly. In the past year, its market share has increased seven percent overall. In addition, it has a very strong hold in the Texas area where it holds close to a 30 percent market share. J.R.'s introduction of another new product will definitely have a negative affect on our market share, both overall and in Texas.	Sam Houston (Salesperson)	Confirmed

Exhibit 7-5

Situation Analysis

This is the most valuable of the analyses prepared in the hierarchy. It is a written report supported by charts, graphs, static numerical information and results of modeling/statistical analyses. It is the detailed support for the special intelligence briefings and should contain the following:

■ Strategic issue

■ Supporting information
  — Product/service
  — Sales/marketing activities
  — Strengths and weaknesses
  — Future plans and strategies

■ Alternative source of action

■ Recommended course of action

This report is usually targeted toward senior management, division management, marketing managers, sales managers and other selected functional managers.

Exhibit 7-5, Continued

Situation Analysis

Example

Recent Key Events

■ Convenience stores in Dallas, Texas are test marketing the new bottle produced by J.R. Industries.

■ J.R. expects to introduce the bottle within 90 days.

■ J.R. has gained seven percent in overall market share in the past year.

■ J.R. already possesses a commanding 30 percent share of the Texas market.

Strategies

■ Identify how J.R. is producing the new bottle and what it would take for us to do the same.

■ Increase research and development efforts to keep up with the competition.

■ Step up marketing efforts of current product lines, especially in the Texas market.

Exhibit 7-5, Continued

Situation Analysis

Overall Sales Strength vs. J.R. Industries

	Our Company	J.R. Industries
Beverage Industry	◑	●
Chemical Industry	●	○
Food Industry	◑	◑

Regional Sales Strength vs. J.R. Industries

	Our Company	J.R. Industries
Western Region of United States	●	◑
Southern Region of United States	◑	●
Midwestern Region of United States	○	◐

Legend: ● Strong ◑ Moderate ○ Weak

Exhibit 7-5, Continued

Situation Analysis

J.R. Industries
Regional Market Share

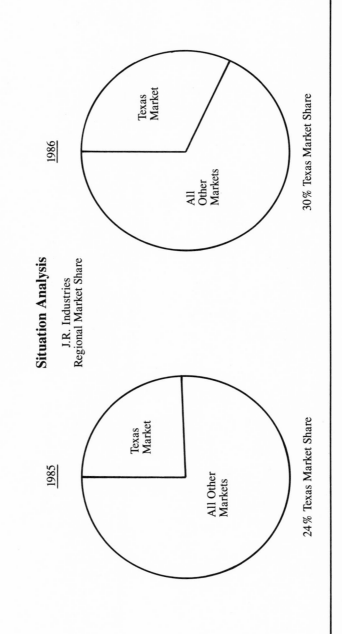

1986

Texas Market

All Other Markets

30% Texas Market Share

1985

Texas Market

All Other Markets

24% Texas Market Share

Exhibit 7-5, Continued

Situation Analysis

J.R. Industries
Overall Market Share

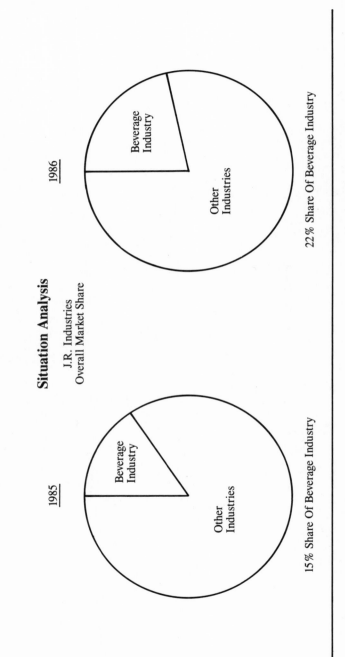

1985

Beverage Industry

Other Industries

15% Share Of Beverage Industry

1986

Beverage Industry

Other Industries

22% Share Of Beverage Industry

Exhibit 7-6

Monthly Intelligence Briefings

Monthly intelligence briefings can include both strategic and tactical information. This is a bound report which would have a few pages of intelligence bullet points followed by copies of articles and interview notes from the month. Depending upon the amount of collected information, this report may optionally be produced on a quarterly basis. Monthly intelligence briefings are usually targeted toward senior management, division management, marketing managers and other selected functional managers.

Exhibit 7-6, Continued

Monthly Intelligence Briefings

Example

Monthly Intelligence Briefing
November, 1986

Page 1

■ Altek's business is gradually improving and the company is currently operating at 75 percent of its capacity. In addition, order backlog for Altek's headsets continues to grow. It now seems that Altek's fear of severe price competition at the low end of the market was premature. (The Daily Journal)

■ Per a source at Altek, the company was operating at 75 percent of its capacity in September. In October, however, the company operated at approximately 80 percent of its capacity. In addition, Altek anticipates operating at close to 100 percent capacity by January of 1987. (Altek Plant Manager)

Subsequent Pages

■ Articles
■ Database searches

Exhibit 7-7

Special Intelligence Briefings

Special intelligence briefings are the highest form of intelligence. They are prepared only when there is a strategic or tactical decision to be made by senior management. They should only be one to two pages in length and should contain the following kinds of information:

- Strategic issue
- Supporting information
- Alternative courses of action
- Recommended course of action

Special intelligence briefings are targeted toward senior management.

Exhibit 7-7, Continued

Special Intelligence Briefings

Example

Special Intelligence Briefing
October 10, 1986

Strategic Issue	Supporting Information	Recommended Strategy	Alternative Strategies
■ J.R. Industries is introducing a two liter tamper-proof beverage container.	■ Convenience stores in Dallas, Texas are test marketing the new bottle. ■ J.R. expects to introduce the bottle within 90 days. ■ J.R. has gained 7% overall market share in the past year. ■ J.R. already possesses a commanding 30 percent share of the Texas market.	■ Identify how J.R. is producing the new bottle and what it would take for us to do the same.	■ Increase research and development efforts to keep up with the competition. ■ Step up marketing efforts of current product lines, especially in the Texas market.

Chapter 8

Designing a Business Intelligence System

The development of a business intelligence system is a complex effort. First, it requires the support of management. It also requires the support of all key personnel in line functions. As explained in Chapter 4, various department managers can make large contributions to the system by supplying information. These same employees can also be instrumental in designing the business intelligence system.

All too frequently companies err by trying to design and install the ideal business intelligence system - one covering all competitors, all products, all markets, all customers and all technology. This approach assuredly leads to failure. It is much better to focus on one situation at a time and string together a series of small successes. This helps to facilitate the strategic change within the organization which is necessary for overall success.

Facilitating strategic change is an ongoing activity which necessitates an ongoing system for gathering and analyzing intelligence. The overall approach to systems development is illustrated in Exhibit 8-1.

Exhibit 8-1

System Development Approach

1. Establish need for function

2. Identify reporting requirements

3. Identify data requirements and sources

4. Gather data and prepare prototype reports

5. Determine approach to mechanization

6. Design and install mechanized system

Establish Need for Function

Start by reviewing your company's strategic plans, organization charts and monthly management reports. The purpose of this exercise is to identify major strategies and areas of emphasis. It also identifies potential providers and users of the intelligence.

Next, identify your key direct competitors. If the initial list is over five in length, "sharpen the pencil". There have been many times that companies state they have 100 - 200 key competitors. This is impossible! In any one served market, there should be no more than five key competitors. Use the 80/20 rule if you are having problems. Identify the 20% of the companies which provide 80% of the competition, and focus on one or a few competitors as you develop your intelligence system. As you assess their relative strengths and weaknesses, identify the competitor that represents the biggest threat.

The next step should be to outline your overall system development approach. A major part of this should include estimating the cost of developing this function as well as the ongoing costs. The development costs represent the cost of designing the system, including any software, hardware and data base subscriptions. Ongoing costs include the payroll cost of the intelligence coordinator(s), data base charges, clipping charges and software development costs.

After completing these planning steps, meet with potential "champions" to pre-sell the concept. Look for key managers in the organization that have the necessary clout to provide support for a business intelligence plan. The specific functional area which you approach is of little importance as long as your audience is comprised of "champions". The intelligence function has been seen in sales, marketing, planning, research & development, and quality assurance.

Senior management approval may not be necessary. After all, most senior managers believe that intelligence gathering is already established within the organization. They assume that someone in the sales and marketing function is coordinating this effort. If they only knew....

Identify Reporting Requirements

As mentioned in Chapter 2, intelligence gathering should focus on key success factors. Ideally, these factors should be translated into measurable key control indicators so that competitive activity can be measured in a quantitative as well as qualitative way. Some key success factors lend themselves to quantitative analysis much more directly than others. For example, if high market share were a key success factor, it is easy to identify a key control indicator. However, measuring a key success factor such as image is more difficult because it is difficult to quantify.

The next step is to determine the basis upon which your company competes in the marketplace. Do you compete on the basis of price, differentiation, focus or some other factors? Your intelligence reports should relate to the basis upon which you compete. For example, if your company does not compete on the basis of price, don't focus the data gathering and reporting effort on competitive prices.

After thinking about the information you want to produce from your system, define the types, levels of detail and frequencies of reports. Monthly reporting is generally best. Quarterly reporting may have very little value because the information may be three months old. Much of the value of intelligence is in its timeliness.

Then develop preliminary report formats with "live" data from one key competitor. Again, it is much easier to sell the concept if you have something tangible to offer. Take your ideas and sample reports to potential users. Discuss the reports with the users and solicit suggestions for enhancement. Exhibit 8-2 illustrates three generic reporting formats which if used will result in a system that has maximum flexibility.

Exhibit 8-2
(Page 1 of 3)

Generic Reporting Formats

Generic Format #1

Date	Source	Reliability*	Intelligence	Impact

*Rumor
Comfirmed Rumor
Fact
Hard Fact

Exhibit 8-2
(Page 2 of 3)

Generic Format #2

	Historical			Information Type	Projected			
	Year 1	Year 2	Year 3	CG %		Year 1	Year 2	Year 3	CG %

Exhibit 8-2
(Page 3 of 3)

Generic Format #3

Information Type	Your Company	Other Companies						
		A	B	C	D	E	F	G

Identify Data Requirements and Sources

This step of the process requires identifying potential data and the alternative sources for each data requirement. A particular piece of information is probably obtainable from both internal and external sources and in published and non-published form. For example, if a company's annual sales were an information requirement, many potential sources are available, including:

- Annual report from company

- Ex-employees

- On-line data bases

- SEC reports

- Competitor employees

- Your employees

- Distributors of competitor products

- Common suppliers

Once you have listed the potential sources of information you can prioritize each potential source and build your network for collecting each piece of information. This process was discussed in detail in previous chapters.

Gather Data and Prepare Prototype Reports

Start by gathering data for one key competitor or customer. Sort the data as it is received and develop a filing system. As one file gets too big, break it down into smaller files. Some of the more common filing systems have a hierarchy as illustrated in Exhibit 8-3. It is best to let your filing system evolve so that it reflects your needs as you progress.

After the initial data gathering is complete, prepare a set of reports, and issue these reports regularly for a period of two to three months. During this time, discuss the reported information with the users to determine their overall satisfaction level.

Repeat this cycle on a continuous basis so that the system continues to provide the needed information. After you are comfortable that you can deliver results for the first company, start the next while you continue with the first. This process significantly reduces the risk of failure.

Determine Approach To Mechanization

Mechanization should be the last step in developing a business intelligence system. Many companies try to mechanize too early in the process. Until you have a good set of manual procedures and files in place, mechanization is not advised. Most of the successful intelligence groups have not built mechanized data bases. Those that have tend to keep them very simple.

When you start to move toward mechanization, you also have to change your mind-set as it relates to computer systems. Decision support systems are flexible tools which enable data to be manipulated in an unstructured manner. They are very different from transaction systems such as payroll or order entry. Business intelligence systems are decision support systems.

Exhibit 8-3

Hierarchical Filing System

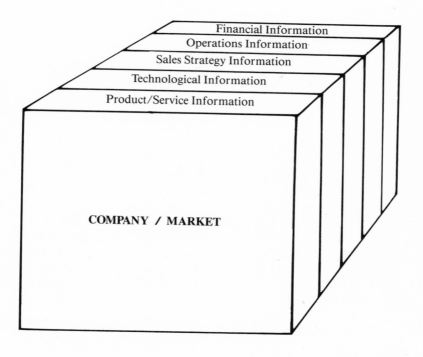

Decision support systems have the following characteristics:

- data base capabilities

- modeling/statistical analysis capabilities

- management reporting capabilities

- graphics capabilities

They consist of fourth generation software tools which allow users to program without technical support. They are used in highly unstructured ways and are developed in an evolutionary fashion.

Develop Evolutionary Approach

Start simple and keep it simple! Begin by using personal computers with word processing, data base and spreadsheet capability. Always use the 80/20 rule when considering mechanization—implement only the 20% of the system that provides 80% of the benefit.

Based on your manual system, develop the tentative data base design using both a top-down and bottom-up approach. The top-down approach consists of determining the categories of information that you want to store. Examples are shown in Exhibit 8-4.

Using these categories, go through an "explosion" or "functional decomposition" process to determine specific data elements to be stored under each category. For example, under the financial category, the explosion may yield sales, cost of sales and gross margin by product for each competitor.

Exhibit 8-4

Top-Down Data Base Design

■ Financial Information

■ Organizational Structure

■ Operations Information

■ Market Information

■ Marketing Information

■ Corporate Information

■ Product Mix Information

■ Corporate Direction

■ Distribution Channel Information

■ Environmental Influences

The "bottom-up" approach consists of brainstorming every possible data element that might be included in the data base. This is somewhat dangerous but, nonetheless, a useful exercise. The danger of the bottom-up approach is that it usually yields a few hundred possible data elements.

Appendix H is a Competitor Profile Checklist that can be used in the bottom-up approach. Appendix I illustrates the results of a data base brainstorming session. For each element, you might want five years of history and five years of projected information. Then, you might want data elements to keep track of the information by market segment, country or world region. When you multiply the number of resulting data elements by the number of companies or products you want to store, it is easy to see that data bases can easily get out of control.

Again, don't try to build the ideal mechanized system that stores everything you want to know about every competitor, customer, product or technology. This is an impossible task. Companies that have taken this approach end up two years later without a system in place and no interim successes along the way.

Review Software and Hardware Alternatives

Data base software and/or word processing software are useful for storing and sorting qualitative information. This software is particularly suited to producing monthly news bulletins, competitor profiles or strategic impact worksheets.

Modeling (spreadsheet) software is best for analyzing and charting quantitative information. The situation analyses and special intelligence briefings can be prepared using this software.

At the time of this writing, no "canned" business intelligence software packages were available. In addition, no fully integrated fourth generation languages were available to build a comprehensive software solution on a microcomputer. Consequently, it is necessary to evaluate the available software and tailor it to your specific intelligence needs.

Look at software before looking at computer hardware. It is the software that provides the functions and features (i.e., reporting and data base capabilities). Develop a functions and features checklist. Down the left hand side of a worksheet list the capabilities that your software must have. Then list the various software packages across the top of the worksheet in columns. This worksheet approach helps you to identify the winners and avoid the losers.

When you have narrowed the field to a few software alternatives, have a software salesperson demonstrate to you that it will indeed work for your application.

After you have selected software, the hardware choice should be simple. You should simply buy the hardware that will accommodate your software selections. Of course, you also should consider factors such as price, service and reliability.

Microcomputers are the best alternative for business intelligence systems. The use of mainframe computers is discouraged unless the primary role of the mainframe is to store information. Minicomputers are fine to the extent that programming support is not required. A business intelligence system should be built, operated and controlled by the end- user. It is not a system to be delegated to the MIS department.

Design and Install Mechanized System

The specific design and installation tasks you must follow depend on the software and hardware selection.

The final steps of developing an operational system include:

- Finalizing report design based on software capabilities

- Finalizing the data base design

- Coding, testing and debugging the system

- Building the data base

- Developing user guidelines and procedures

- Producing the first set of mechanized reports

Again, you're not finished when the first set of reports is produced. This is a decision support system. Continually re-evaluate the reports and the overall system design.

Chapter 9 will discuss the organizational issues in developing a business intelligence function.

Chapter 9

Organizing a Business Intelligence Function

Organizing the business intelligence function can be difficult to accomplish. The first constraint is usually one of cost. Most companies prefer not to devote resources to a function until it can be proven that the function is necessary and will succeed.

The next problem is one of finding a "champion" that has enough clout to facilitate change in the organization. This is usually the "fast tracker" within management at the corporate or business unit level. Finally, the concept of business intelligence must be sold to those in the organization that will provide information to the system.

This chapter discusses the analysis of staffing needs, presents typical organization charts and budgets for the function, and further discusses how the concept can be sold within the organization.

Set Objectives

Begin by establishing the overall objectives for the function for a three to five year time frame. Most intelligence groups find that it takes this long for the function to evolve. Be wary of setting objectives for the first year which cannot be achieved. Remember, it is better to start small and build on success. Some typical first year objectives might include:

■ Monitor two to three key competitors on a continuous basis.

■ Establish the intelligence coordinator role.

■ Develop a manual data base for competitors.

■ Issue news bulletins, strategic impact worksheets and intelligence briefings on companies being monitored.

■ Begin active solicitation of intelligence from both internal and external sources.

The evolving nature of the function suggests that in later years the objectives must be broadened. For example, you should continue to add additional companies at a rate which can be supported by the staffing levels you select. As the intelligence staff becomes more efficient they are able to support the addition of more companies without increasing the staff.

Analysis of Staffing Needs

Based on the objectives you have outlined for the function, determine the primary tasks to be performed and the amount of time required to perform each task. The tasks usually include some combination of those listed in Exhibit 9-1.

Exhibit 9-1

Tasks Required of Intelligence Personnel

- Gathering information via telephone from internal company personnel

- Gathering information via telephone from external company personnel

- Reading and summarizing clippings

- Performing on-line data base searches

- Interacting with internal company personnel

- Analyzing information for strategic and/or tactical significance

- Preparing periodic reports

- Presenting findings to management

- Responding to ad hoc inquiries

Once the tasks are identified, determine the mix of part-time and full-time personnel. The mix is substantially different for the initial stages. Initial data gathering is usually done with part-time resources. Ongoing activities usually require at least one full-time coordinator.

Based on the tasks and resources, determine the background that full-time candidates should have. A marketing or planning employee who understands the markets in which you compete would be an ideal candidate. However, the most important characteristics of a candidate are communication skills, motivation and enthusiasm—and curiosity.

Although industry experience is sometimes a plus, it is definitely not necessary. The functional skills of data gathering, organizing and communicating far outweigh the benefits industry experience might offer. In fact, in most telephone interviews, it is better if you are not an expert; knowing too much closes the door on many potential sources.

Small Companies vs. Large

Intelligence gathering is not any different for small companies than for large organizations. However, the functional organization needed to collect intelligence in large companies is more complex.

Intelligence Function - The Small Organization

Small companies achieve success when they assign the coordinator role to the Vice President of Marketing. Figure 9-1 illustrates the intelligence function for the small organization. Information is actively gathered and analyzed by this individual. With only one coordinating point, a great amount of control can be exercised over the function. The only additional coordination required is with the Vice President of Sales, if that position exists.

Figure 9-1

Intelligence Function - Small Organization

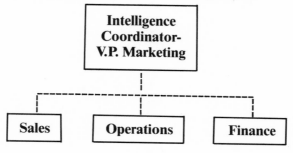

The Vice President of Marketing utilizes part-time resources to accomplish the gathering and analyzing of information. This person actively solicits input from employees in sales, operations and financial areas of the organization. His or her budget usually does not include full-time people. The only incremental budget consideration is the cost of third-party research and clipping services.

Intelligence Function - The Large Organization

In the case of the large organization, the actual level in the organization for the intelligence coordinator should coincide with strategic planning efforts. For example, if the organization does its strategic planning using a large centralized strategic planning function, the competitor intelligence function will probably work best if centralized. Most companies have gone away from the large central organization for planning and prefer to develop plans at the level in the organization where they must be implemented. If this is the case, this approach should be used for the business intelligence function as well.

The large organization presents a more difficult coordinating role. The organization chart is similar to the small organization but is multiplied by the number of distinct business units comprising the total organization. This in turn necessitates a central coordinating point. This is illustrated in Figure 9-2.

Figure 9-2

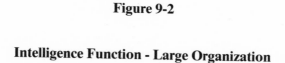

Intelligence Function - Large Organization

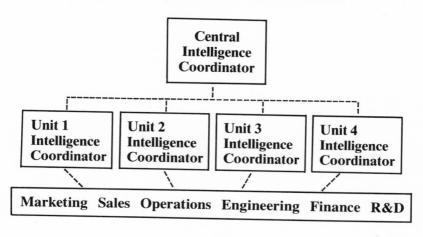

In the first year it is best if each of the unit intelligence coordinators work independently. The central intelligence coordinator role becomes more important when the gathering performed at the lower levels becomes more broad based.

Hundreds of observations over the years suggest that the intelligence function tends to bring business units together and sometimes dissolves the rivalries that exist. This happens because everyone realizes the importance of ongoing business intelligence and they realize that much can be gained by sharing their resources to achieve a common end.

The recommended approach in large organizations is to initially develop a "quiet, private network" of individuals that want to participate in the intelligence function. Forget the fanfare such as a formal announcement by the CEO that this function is being established. Don't include this function in each managers' MBO's. Don't include these responsibilities in the job descriptions of employees. You initially want to develop an informal team of people that participate because they want to and not because they have to.

Developing the "quiet, private intelligence network" takes time and essentially requires figuratively re-drawing the organization charts of the company. For example, you want to find those individuals in each business unit that are enthusiastic, aggressive, curious and want to participate in the network. These individuals may be as many as 10 levels below management. The managers in each of these 10 levels may not want their subordinate participating in the network unless the manager is controlling it. You can begin to see the potential political problems. This is the primary reason for the "quiet, private" approach at least in the initial stages.

The best intelligence comes directly from the source. Ten layers of review usually results in good intelligence being watered down or filtered out. You need information directly from the source so that it can be analyzed for intelligence purposes.

To the extent possible, the intelligence coordinator should be a full-time resource. In large organizations, an intelligence function with all "part-timers" seldom works. It is recommended that one full-time unit coordinator be selected in the initial stages followed by others as the function evolves.

A typical start-up budget for a large organization is illustrated in Exhibit 9-2.

Exhibit 9-2

Start-up Budget For a Large Organization

Salaries and Benefits	$ 60,000
Microcomputer and Software	10,000
External Data Base Charges	12,000
External Clipping Charges	6,000
External Research	12,000
	$100,000

Large companies on average spend $500,000 per year for their intelligence function. The range is $100,000 to as much as $5,000,000. Clearly, the companies spending millions of dollars recognize the importance of the function.

The Use of Third Parties

The use of third parties is recommended to further maximize the time of the coordinator. For example, clipping services can clip articles on a more cost effective basis than trying to perform this task internally.

Intelligence firms can also be helpful in accelerating the process of information gathering and analysis. They can perform the more difficult information gathering tasks or assist at a higher level in the design of the intelligence system and training of employees.

Selling the Concept Within the Organization

Many advantages become apparent in a formalized business intelligence system. First, it facilitates a more efficient use of limited resources. The concept of one coordinator leveraging his or her time by involving others in the process is a major selling point. Secondly, an intelligence system leads a company to act rather than react to events in the marketplace and helps a company capitalize on opportunities. Lastly, it helps business unit managers increase their overall understanding of the business and the ways in which it can achieve a competitive advantage.

However, with all of these advantages, support is difficult to obtain until management has seen results or understands what can reasonably be expected from a business intelligence system. Unfortunately, it is a "catch 22" situation.

The selling of the business intelligence concept should be done in steps as the system evolves. It is difficult, if not impossible, to sell the entire concept in the beginning. Many managers believe this function is already being accomplished somewhere in the organization. These managers usually don't see the value of a more coordinated business intelligence function.

The best way to sell the concept is to show a series of successes. Steady, positive results over a period of time enable you to string together a series of small successes. This illustrates the importance of the function to managers who may not initially appreciate the value of a coordinated approach.

The ultimate selling point is demonstrating that the system has enabled your organization to stay one step ahead of the competition.

Chapter 10

Guarding Your Company Secrets

No intelligence book is complete without a discussion of the flip-side of intelligence work—guarding your secrets. After reading this book, you should be keenly aware that your own company's secrets are at risk.

Guarding your secrets is a matter of managing your risk. The nature of the risk depends on:

- The scope and scale of materials and documents your competitors might want

- The type of business involved

- The size and success of the business

- The type of competition they represent

The effort and expense you allocate to security should be based on the overall risk you perceive. For example, you purchase insurance to cover specific risks. The cost of that insurance depends on the coverage you select. Your coverage coincides with your perceived or actual level of risk.

Many forces are at work in marketing research and industrial espionage, including employees and professionals. The list of employees might include:

■ "Loyal" employees

■ The temporary employee

■ The enthusiastic braggart

■ The employee with a grudge

Loyal employees may be divulging confidential information, either knowingly or unknowingly. Temporary employees have no company loyalty so are apt to disclose information to outsiders without knowing of the strategic significance. Enthusiastic braggarts are probably the most common. They are employees who love their job and like to tell others the most intimate details of what they do. Finally, employees with a grudge might do almost anything.

Professionals in the intelligence (or espionage) business may include the following:

■ Internal "Plants"

■ Internal "Sleepers"

■ False head-hunters

■ Eavesdroppers

Internal "plants" are individuals that are planted within your organization with the sole objective of stealing trade secrets. There have been hundreds of reported cases involving plants. Internal "sleepers" are another version of plants. They are planted in an organization, are loyal employees for a period of time, and then they begin to divulge company secrets.

A variety of techniques are used by espionage professionals in gathering information:

- Posing as visitors, contractors, students and journalists

- Collecting trash

- Bar conversations

- Bribery and threats

- Optical aids

- Audio aids

Using a disguise is the most common technique. For example, a large number of people pose as students. Collecting trash is not as common but occasionally practiced when the stakes are high. Bar conversations are common, especially at trade shows and local bars near a competitor's operations. Bribery and threats are not widely practiced. Optical and audio aids, however, are more common than most people think. It was reported that the FBI uncovers thousands of "bugs" in businesses every year.

Companies often assume that that their competition will go to almost any length to gather information. They make an assumption, however, that the competition will not resort to anything illegal. This is not necessarily true.

Case Example

A senior executive has just dictated to his secretary some extremely sensitive information about the company. In what ways is this information accessible by outsiders who want to steal it?

Solution

1. The man

2. The secretary

3. A bug in the phone

4. A bug in the furniture or wall

5. The shorthand notebook used

6. The typewriter ribbon used

7. A spoiled photocopy or computer printout in the waste-basket

8. A boom mike directed at the window

9. Photography by telephoto lens from a nearby office

10. A copy in an unlocked filing cabinet

11. The photographing, copying or theft of a copy by cleaning or maintenance personnel

Unfortunately, the legal remedies are usually unsatisfactory. Laws on stealing trade secrets, invading the privacy of others and trespassing are on the books. However, unless you actually catch someone with their hands in the filing cabinet, watch them take documents out of the building and have them arrested at that point, little or no recourse is available to you.

Even if the laws were substantial it is unclear whether this stops those people who want your information. For example, people purchase elaborate security systems for their automobile to protect themselves from the risk of car theft. Everyone knows that stealing a car is illegal but the law itself does not prevent those who wish to steal your car from doing so.

The bottom line is preventive medicine!

Many things can be done to protect your organization from losing confidential or other proprietary information. A few of these are listed in Exhibit 10-1.

Exhibit 10-1

Company Safeguards

■ Establish a security committee.

■ Review existing security procedures.

■ Analyze risk in all divisions/departments.

■ Develop security guidelines.

■ Train all employees.

■ Conduct ongoing security audits.

If a security committee is not in existence, one should be established. The first task of this committee should be to review the current security procedures and analyze the risk or potential risk in every area of the organization.

The review should be thorough and should encompass all areas of the organization. The security of the physical premises should include searching for signs of previous breaches, especially sensitive areas such as the company boardroom and conference rooms. Entrance and perimeter protection should be checked by experts in the field and possibly tested to ensure that the procedures are followed.

Specialized procedures for internal areas containing sensitive information should be reviewed. Many times audit firms perform a review of internal controls related to electronic data processing as part of the audit function. The results of these audits should be reviewed and the problems noted should be acted upon. The same procedures used for EDP controls audits can be expanded and used for other areas containing sensitive information.

The procedures used to verify pre-employment history should be reviewed. In addition to the standard pre-employment checks, tests can be administered to recruits which help evaluate the recruit's propensity toward theft, substance abuse, violence and other habits unfavorable to the company or the working environment.

The way in which you dispose of important information is of equal or greater importance than the way you store it. Shredders and other devices should be used to reduce the risk of information being leaked. Old computer tapes and word processing disks should be destroyed or altered in such a manner that the information they once contained cannot be re-constructed.

Based on this review and analysis, security guidelines should be developed. These security guidelines should not be of the three-ring binder type. Rather, they should be a list not more than one page long. An example is shown in Exhibit 10-2.

Exhibit 10-2

Example Security Guidelines

1. Don't talk about company business in elevators, restaurants or other public places.

2. Be very careful about what you are saying and to whom you are saying it.

3. Don't provide information of any kind over the telephone unless it is information which already appears in published form.

4. Confidential or proprietary information should not be discussed with anyone, including relatives and friends.

5. Desk drawers and file cabinets should be locked at the close of business each day.

6. Visitors should be escorted as they move through the building, even if they are just going to the restroom.

7. If you encounter a stranger in your area, ask them their business.

A simple set of security guidelines is easily developed and communicated to all employees. The three-inch binder prepared by the company security department seldom works. Likewise, sophisticated techniques or gadgetry such as magnetically encoded I.D. cards don't work without the cooperation of all employees. The best approach is to keep security guidelines simple for maximum effectiveness.

Security audits should be conducted from time to time. They should not be conducted for the purpose of firing people. Rather, they should be conducted to identify potential leaks. A positive approach to security audits sells the overall importance of them. An example of a security audit plan is shown in Appendix J.

The audit plan should test every possible disguise that someone might use to obtain trade secrets. This means using unethical techniques that you definitely would not use in your own business intelligence gathering for the purpose of strategic and tactical planning. The results of the security audit can then be used to refine the security guidelines and improve employee training.

In conclusion we offer these final pearls of wisdom: 1) Prevention is always better than the cure, 2) Security does not work without the ongoing commitment of senior management and support of all employees, and 3) A simple set of guidelines and a disciplined approach to training are necessary to ensure successful security.

Chapter 11

Putting It All Together

This book has presented the "how-to's" of business intelligence: How to gather, sort, analyze and synthesize information for strategic and tactical decision-making purposes. Your use of this book should help you to accelerate the business intelligence process within your company.

Exhibit 11-1 presents an action plan that you can tailor to your specific situation. A detailed version of this plan is in Appendix K. Using this plan should help to ensure a successful start-up or refinement of your intelligence function.

Business intelligence is here to stay. It is a function that was virtually unheard of in the 1970s. In the 1990s it will be necessary for market survival. Ongoing strategic decisions will require a continuous stream of information. A business intelligence system will provide that stream of information if organized properly. Those companies that are able to integrate business intelligence with strategic decision making will be the winners in their industry, and the employees responsible for organizing the intelligence function will be the heroes.

Exhibit 11-1

Summary Action Plan

  I. Establish need for function

  II. Identify reporting requirements

  III. Identify data requirements and sources of information

  IV. Gather data and prepare prototype reports

  V. Determine staffing requirements

  VI. Determine approach to mechanization

  VII. Design and install mechanized system

Appendix

Appendix A

Industry Sources
Health Care

American Hospital Association Guide to the Healthcare Field. Chicago: American Hospital Publishing 1986.

American Hospital Association Statistics. American Chicago: Hospital Publishing, 1986.

Annotated Bibliography of Health Economics, English Language Sources. Anthony J. Culyer, ed. New York: St. Martins Press, 1977.

Canadian Hospital Directory. (annual) Eleanor Sawyer, ed. Ottawa, Ontario.

Directory of Medical Specialists, 22nd Edition, 1985-86, Volume 1. Chicago: Marquis Who's Who.

Drug Information for the Health Care Provider, Sixth Edition 1986. Rockville, Maryland: The United States Pharmacopoeial Convention, Inc., 1985.

Encyclopedia of Health: Information Source, First Edition. Paul Wasserman, ed. Detroit: Gale Research Company, 1986.

Encyclopedia of Medical Organizations and Agencies, Second Edition. Anthony T. Kruzas, ed. Detroit: Gale Research Company, 1986.

Handbook of Resolutions and Decisions of the World Health Assembly and the Executive Board, Volume II, 1972-1984. Geneva: World Health Organization, 1985.

Healthcare Administration: A Guide to Information Sources. Dwight A. Morris. Detroit: Gale Research Company, 1978.

Healthcare Costs and Financing. Rita M. Keintz. Detroit: Gale Research Company, 1981.

Healthcare Statistics: A Guide to Information Sources. Freida O. Weise. Detroit: Gale Research Company, 1980.

Health Information Systems, A Bibliography. Donald G. Ziegenfuss and James T. Ziegenfuss, Jr. New York: IFI/Plenum Data Company. 1984.

Health and Medical Economics: A Guide to Information Sources. Ackroyd Tid. Detroit: Gale Research Company, 1977.

Health Organizations of the United States, Canada and the World, Fifth Edition. Paul Wasserman, ed. Detroit: Gale Research Company, 1981.

Health Services Directory. Anthony T. Kruzas, ed. Detroit, Michigan: Gale Research Company.

Health Services in the United States, Second Edition. Florence A. Wilson, M.D. Cambridge, Massachusetts: Ballinger Publishing Company, 1985.

Hospital Literature Index. (quarterly) Chicago: American Hospital Publishing, 1986.

The Hospitals and Health Services Yearbook and Directory of Hospital Suppliers. (annual) N.W. Chaplin, ed. London: The Institute of Health Service Administrators.

HPG Hospital Purchasing Guide 1986. Curtis S. Risley, ed. Fort Washington, Pennsylvania: IMS Communications, Inc., 1986.

HSP/85, Hospital Survey Profile. Joint Commission on Accreditation of Hospitals.

Index Medicus. (monthly) Bethesda, Maryland: National Library of Medicine.

Index to Scientific & Technical Proceedings. (monthly) Philadelphia: Institute for Scientific Information, Inc., 1986.

International Dictionary of Medicine and Biology. New York: John Wiley & Sons, 1986.

International Medical Who's Who, Second Edition. Longman Group Limited, 1985.

Introduction to Reference Sources in the Health Sciences. Fred W. Roper. Chicago: Chicago Medical Library Association, 1980.

Medical Device Register, Volume 1—U.S. & Canada, 1986. Stamford, Connecticut: Directory Systems, Inc., 1986.

Medical and Health Care Books and Serials in Print, 1986, An Index to Literature in the Health Sciences, Volume 1. New York: Reed Publishing USA, 1986.

The Medical and Healthcare Marketplace Guide. Adeline B. Hale and Arthur B. Hale, eds. Miami: International Bio-Medical Information Service, Inc., 1986.

Medical and Health Information Directory, Volume 1: Organizations, Agencies and Institutions, Third Edition. Anthony T. Kruzas, Kay Gill, Karen Backus, eds. Detroit: Gale Research Company, 1985.

Medical and Health Information Volume 2: Libraries, Publications, Audiovisual and Data Base Services, Third Edition. Anthony T. Kruzas, Kay Gill, Karen Backus, eds. Detroit: Gale Research Company, 1985.

Medical and Health Information Volume 3: Anthony T. Kruzas, Kay Gill, Karen Backus, eds. Detroit: Gale Research Company, 1985.

The Medical Research Directory. New York: John Wiley & Sons, 1983.

Medline: A Basic Guide to Searching. Susan J. Feinglos. Chicago: Medical Library Association, Inc. 1985.

National Council for International Health. (monthly) Washington, D.C.: National Council for International Health.

The Saunders Health Care Directory 84/85. Philadelphia: Norback & Company, Inc., 1984.

Selected List of Books and Journals for the Small Medical Library 1983/84 Edition. Alfred N. Brandon. Chicago: Login Brothers Book Company.

SRIM Index. (quarterly) Springfield, Virginia: National Technical Information Service.

Trade Names Dictionary, Fifth Edition, 1986-87. Donna Wood, ed. Detroit: Gale Research Company, 1986.

The U.S. Health System, Origins and Functions, Second Edition. Marshall W. Raffel, Ph.D. New York: John Wiley & Sons, 1984.

Who's Who in Biotechnology, 5th Edition. Woodbridge, Connecticut: Research Publications, 1986.

Who's Who in Health Care, Second Edition, 1981. Rockville, Maryland: Aspen Publications, 1981.

World Directory of Medical Schools, Fifth Edition. Geneva: World Health Organization, 1979.

Appendix B

Industry Sources Telecommunications

Administration of American Telecommunications Policy, Volume 1. John M. Kittross, ed. New York: Arno Press, 1980.

An Analysis of the Federal Communications Commission's Group Ownership Rules, January, 1984. Santa Monica, California: Rand.

ATT Bell Laboratories Record. (bi-monthly) Short Hills, New Jersey: ATT.

Breaking Up Bell. Essays on Industrial Organization and Regulation. David S. Evans, ed. New York: Elsevier Science Publishing Co., Inc., 1983.

Communications Daily. Washington, D.C.: T.V. Digest Publishing.

Communications News. Geneva, Illinois: Harcourt, Bruce, Jovanovich, Inc.

Communications Policy for National Development. A Comparative Perspective. London: Routledge & Kegan Paul, Ltd.

Communications Policy and the Political Process. John J. Havick, ed. Westport, Connecticut: Greenwood Press, 1983.

Communications/Systems Equipment Design. New York, New York: McGraw-Hill, Inc.

Communications Week. Manhasset, New York: CMP Publications.

The Competitor for Markets in International Telecommunications. Ronald S. Eward. Dedham, Massachusetts: Artech House, Inc., 1984.

Data Communications. Hightstown, New Jersey: Mc Graw-Hill, Inc.

Datapro Reports on Telecommunications. Delran, New Jersey: Datapro Research Corporation.

The Deregulation of International Telecommunications. Ronald Eward. Dedham, Massachusetts: Artech House, Inc., 1985.

Documents in American Telecommunications Policy, Volume One. John M. Kittros, ed. New York: Arno Press, 1977.

Electronic Business Communications. Denver, Colorado: Cahners Publishing Company.

Electronic Communications Systems. William C. House, ed. New York: PBI, A Petrocelli Book.

Fiber Optics and Communications. Boston: Information Gatekeepers, Inc.

Hermes Bound. The Policy and Technology of Telecommunications. Clare D. McGillem and William P. McLauchlan. West Lafayette, Indiana: Purdue University, 1978.

International Telecommunications and Information Policy. Christopher H. Sterling, ed. Washington, D.C.: Communications Press, Inc., 1984.

Introduction to Business Telecommunications. George W. Reynolds. Columbus, Ohio: Charles E. Merrill Publishing Company, 1984.

Issues in International Telecommunications Policy: A Sourcebook. Jane H. Yurow, ed. Washington, D.C.: The George Washington University, 1983.

Journal of Telecommunication Networks. Rockville, Maryland: Computer Science Press, Inc.

Legal Aspects of Selected Issues in Telecommunications. Stephen B. Perlman. Montvale, New Jersey: Afips Press, 1970.

1985 Mobile Radio Handbook. Maribeth Harper, ed. Denver, Colorado: Titsch Communications, Inc., 1984.

Modern Electronic Communication Techniques. Harold B. Killen. New York: MacMillan Publishing Company, 1985.

New Systems and Services in Telecommunications. G. Cantraine and J. Destine, eds. New York: North-Holland Publishing Company, 1981.

Policy Research in Telecommunications. Vincent Mosco, ed. Norwood, New Jersey: Ablex Publishing Corporation, 1984.

Power of Speech: A History of Standard Telephones and Cables: 1883-1983. Peter Young. London: George Allen & Unwin, Ltd. 1983.

Report to the Congress of the United States: Legislative and Regulatory Actions Needed to Deal with a Changing Domestic Telecommunications Industry. United States General Accounting Office.

The 1986 Satellite Direction, 8th Annual Edition. (annual) Mark R. Kimmel, ed. Potomac, Maryland: Phillips Publishing, Inc., 1986.

Signals The Telephone and Beyond. John R. Pierce. San Francisco: W.H. Freemand and Company, 1981.

Standard & Poor's Industry Surveys. (quarterly) New York: Standard & Poor's Corporation.

Telecom Times & Trends. Mont Vernon, New Hampshire: Frank Communications Group.

Telecommunications. Dedham, Massachusetts: Horizon House.

Telecommunications Access and Public Policy. Norwood, New Jersey: Ablex Publishing Corporation, 1984.

Telecommunications Alert. New York, New York: Management Telecommunications Publishing.

Telecommunications America, Markets Without Boundaries. Manley Rutherford Irwin. Westport, Connecticut: Quorum Books, 1984.

Telecommunications and Economic Development. Virginia deHaven Hitchcock, ed. Washington, D.C.: International Bank for Reconstruction and Development, 1983.

The Telecommunications Industry. The Dynamics of Market Structure. Gerald W. Brock. Cambridge, Massachusetts: Harvard University Press, 1981.

Telecommunications Management. A Practical Approach. New York: AMA Membership Publications Division, 1984.

Telecommunications Policy Handbook. New York: Praeger Publishers, 1982.

Telecommunications and Productivity. Mitchell L. Moss, ed. Reading, Massachusetts: Addison-Wesley Publishing Company, 1981.

Telecommunications Regulation Today and Tomorrow. Eli M. Noam, ed. New York: Harcourt, Brace, Jovanovich Publishing, 1983.

Telecommunications Reports. Washington, D.C.: Business Research Publications, Inc.

Telecommunications Systems and Services Directory, Second Edition. Martin Connors, ed. Detroit, Michigan: Gale Research Company, 1985.

Telecommunications in the U.S.: Trends and Policies. Leonard Lewin, ed. Dedham, Massachusetts: Artech House, Inc., 1981.

The Teleconferencing Resources Directory, 1983-84, First Edition. Ellen A. Lazer, ed. White Plains, New York: Knowledge Industry Publications, Inc., 1983.

Teleconnect. New York, New York: Telecom Library, Inc.

Telephone Engineer & Management. Geneva, Illinois: Harcourt, Brace, Jovanovich, Inc.

Telephony. Chicago, Illinois: Telephony Publishing Corp.

Trends in Communication Regulations. Boston: Econ & Tech, Inc.

The Wired Society. James Martin. Englewood Cliffs, New Jersey: Prentice-Hall, Inc., 1978.

Appendix C

Industry Sources
Banking

ABA Banking Journal. (monthly) New York, New York: Simmons-Boardman Publishing Corporation.

ABA Banker's Weekly. (weekly newspaper) Washington, DC: American Bankers Association.

American Banker. (daily newspaper) New York, New York: American Banker.

American Bankers Association (ABA) Retail Banker. (monthly newsletter) Washington, DC: American Bankers Association.

Analysis of (year) Bank Marketing Expenditures. (annual) Washington, DC: Bank Marketing Association.

AP-Dow Jones Bankers Report. New York, New York: Dow Jones & Company, Inc.

Bank Administration. (monthly) Rolling Meadows, Illinois: Bank Administration Institute.

Bank Auditing & Accounting Report. (monthly report) Boston, Massachusetts: Warren, Gorham & Lamont, Incorporated.

Bank Automation Newsletter. (monthly) Boston, Massachusetts: Warren, Gorham & Lamont, Incorporated.

Bank Board Letter. (monthly newsletter) St. Louis, Missouri: Director Publications, Incorporated.

Bank Director's Report. (monthly newsletter) Boston, Massachusetts: Warren, Gorham & Lamont, Incorporated.

Banker. (monthly journal) New York, New York: Financial Times Business Information Ltd.

Bankers Almanac and Year Book. (annual directory) New York, New York: Thomas Skinner Directories.

Banker's Letter of the Law. (monthly newsletter) Boston, Massachusetts: Warren, Gorham & Lamont, Incorporated.

Bankers Magazine. (bi-monthly magazine) Boston, Massachusetts: Warren, Gorham & Lamont, Incorporated.

Bank Executive's Report. (semi-monthly report) Boston, Massachusetts: Warren, Gorham & Lamont, Incorporated.

Bank Fact Book. (book) Washington, DC: American Bankers Association.

Bank Insurance & Protection Bulletin. (monthly newsletter) Washington, DC: American Bankers Association.

Banking Law Journal. (monthly magazine) Boston, Massachusetts: Warren, Gorham & Lamont, Incorporated.

Bank Loan Officers Report. (monthly report) Boston, Massachusetts: Warren, Gorham & Lamont, Incorporated.

Bank Marketing. (monthly magazine) Chicago, Illinois. Bank Marketing Association.

Bank Marketing Report. (monthly report) Boston, Massachusetts: Warren, Gorham & Lamont, Incorporated.

Bank Operations Report. (monthly report) Boston, Massachusetts: Warren, Gorham & Lamont, Incorporated.

Bank Personnel News. (bi-monthly newsletter) Washington, DC: American Bankers Association.

Bank Personnel Report. (monthly report) Boston, Massachusetts: Warren, Gorham & Lamont, Incorporated.

Bank Security Report. (monthly report) Boston, Massachusetts: Warren, Gorham & Lamont, Incorporated.

Directory and Guide to the Mutual Savings Banks of the United States. (annual) New York, New York: National Association of Mutual Savings Bank.

Directory of American Savings and Loan Associations. (annual) Baltimore, Maryland: T. K. Sanderson Organization, 1955.

Directory of Trust Institutions. (annual) New York, New York: Fiduciary Publishers, 1959.

Directory of U.S. Banking Executives. New York, New York: American Banker, 1980.

Dow Jones International Banking Wire. (continuous service) New York, New York: Dow Jones & Company, Incorporated.

Encyclopedia of Banking & Finance—7th Edition. Boston, Massachusetts: Banker's Publishing, 1973.

Federal Reserve Bulletin. (monthly) U.S. Governors of the Federal Reserve System.

Financial Advertising Report. (annual report) New York, New York: Media Records, Inc.

Financial Handbook, 5th Edition. (book) New York, New York: Jules Bogen and Samuel Shipman, John Wiley & Sons, Incorporated.

Financial Institutions, Financial Statistics. (quarterly magazine) Ottawa, Ontario, Canada: Statistics Canada.

Financial Market Survey. (newsletter) London, England: Barclay's Bank.

Illinois Banker. (monthly magazine) Chicago, Illinois: Illinois Bankers Association.

Journal of Banking & Finance. (quarterly journal) New York, New York: Elsevier/North-Holland, Inc.

Journal of Money, Credit & Banking. Columbus, Ohio:

Moody's Bank and Finance Manual and News Reports. New York, New York: Moody's Investors Service, Incorporated.

Mortgage Banking. (monthly) Washington, D.C.: Mortgage Bankers Association of America.

Munn's Encyclopedia of Banking and Finance, 8th Edition. (book) Boston, Massachusetts: Bankers Publishing Company, State University Press.

Polk's Daily Bank Information Service. (daily newsletter) Nashville, Tennessee: R. L. Polk & Company.

Polk's World-Bank Directory. (semi-annual directory) Nashville, Tennessee: R. L. Polk & Company.

Polk's World Bank Directory—International Edition. (annual book) Nashville, Tennessee: R. L. Polk & Company.

Polk's World Bank Directory—North American Edition. Nashville, Tennessee: R. L. Polk & Company.

Rand McNally International Bankers Directory. (semiannual directory) Chicago, Illinois: Rand McNally & Company.

Savings Institutions. (monthly) Chicago, Illinois: U.S. League of Savings Institutions.

S & L Sourcebook. Chicago, Illinois: U.S. S&L League, 1954.

The World of Banking. (bi-monthly) Rolling Meadows, Illinois: Bank Administration Institute.

Thruput. (monthly newsletter) Washington, DC: American Bankers Association.

Washington Financial Reports. (loose-leaf books) Washington, DC: Bureau of National Affairs, Incorporated.

Who Owns What in World Banking. (annual) London: Financial Times Business Publishing, Ltd.

Who's Who in Banking. (book) New York, New York: Taplinger Publishing Company.

Who's Who in Finance, 2nd Edition. (publication) Farnborough, Hampshire, England: Gower Publishing Company, Ltd..

Who's Who in Finance and Industry. (biennial book) Chicago, Illinois: Marquis Publications.

Appendix D

Industry Sources
Insurance

Argus F.C. & S. Chart. Cincinnati, Ohio: National Underwriter Company.

Argus Health Chart. Cincinnati, Ohio: National Underwriter Company.

Best's Insurance Management Reports. L/H & P/C. (weekly) Oldwick, New Jersey: A.M. Best Company, Incorporated.

Best's Review L/H & P/C. (monthly) Oldwick, New Jersey: A.M. Best Company, Incorporated.

Business Insurance, 5th edition. Edwin H. White. Englewood Cliffs, New Jersey: Prentice Hall, Incorporated.

Business Insurance. (weekly) New York, New York: Crain Communications.

Council Review. (monthly) Washington, D.C.: American Council of Life Insurance.

CPCU Journal. (quarterly) Malvern Pennsylvania: Society of Chartered Property and Casualty Underwriters.

Dictionary of Insurance. Totowa, New Jersey: Rowman & Allanheld, 1983.

Disability Income & Health Insurance Time Saver. Cincinnati, Ohio: National Underwriter Company.

Employee Benefit Plan Review. (monthly) Chicago, Illinois: Charles D. Spencer & Associates, Incorporated.

Employee Benefits. Washington, D.C.: Chamber of Commerce of the United States.

Employee Benefits Journal. (quarterly) Brookfield, Wisconsin: International Foundation of Employee Benefit Plans.

Estate Planning. (bi-monthly) New York, New York: Warren, Gorham & LaMont.

Financial Planner. (monthly) Atlanta, Georgia: International Association of Financial Planners.

Group Life and Health Insurance. Robert W. Batten. Roswell, Georgia: Professional Book Distributors, 1979.

Health Insurance Underwriter. (monthly) Washington, D.C.: National Association of Health Underwriters.

Information Management in Insurance Companies. Raymond McLeod, Jr.. Roswell, Georgia: Professional Book Distributors, 1985.

Insurance Advocate. (weekly) New York, New York: Roberts Publishing Corporation.

Insurance Almanac. Englewood, New Jersey: Underwriter Printing & Publishing Company.

Insurance Facts. New York, New York: Insurance Information Institute.

Insurance Industry Newsletter. Louisville, Kentucky: Insurance Field Company.

Insurance Periodicals Index. NILS Publishing Company.

Insurance and Employee Benefits Literature. (bi-monthly) Special Libraries Association, Insurance and Employee Benefits Division.

Insurance Review. (monthly) New York, New York: Insurance Information Institute.

Journal of Insurance Regulation. Kansas City, Missouri: NAIC.

Journal of Risk and Insurance. (monthly) Athens, Georgia: American Risk and Insurance Association.

Journal of the American Society of CLU (CLU Journal). (bi-monthly) Bryn Mawr, Pennsylvania. American Society of CLU.

Law and the Life Insurance contract, 5th edition. Roswell, Georgia: Professional Book Distributors, 1984.

Life and Health Insurance Companies as Financial Institutions. Mark R. Greene. Roswell, Georgia: Professional Book Distributors, 1984.

Life and Health Insurance Handbook. Davis W. Gregg and Vane B. Lucas. Homewood, Illinois: Richard D. Irwin, Incorporated, 1973.

Life Association News. (monthly) Washington, D.C.: National Association of Life Underwriters.

Life Insurance, 10th edition. S.S. Huebner and Kenneth Black. Englewood Cliffs, New Jersey: Prentice Hall Incorporated, 1982.

Life Insurance Fact Book. Washington, D.C.: American Council of Life Insurance.

Marketing Life and Health Insurance. Nancy E. Strickler. Roswell, Georgia: Professional Book Distributors, 1981.

Mortgage Investing by Life Insurance Companies. Edward M. Burgh. Roswell, Georgia: Professional Book Distributors, 1983.

NAII Greenbook: Compilation of Property-Casualty Insurance Statistics. Des Plaines, Illinois: National Association of Independent Insurers.

National Underwriter. (weekly) Cincinnati, Ohio: National Underwriter Company.

National Directory of State Agencies. Bethesda, Maryland: National Standards Association.

NICO Newsletter. Alexandria, Virginia: National Insurance Consumer Organization.

Operations of Life and Health Insurance Companies. Kenneth Huggins. Roswell, Georgia: Professional book Distributors, 1986.

Pensions & Investment Age. (bi-weekly) Chicago, Illinois: Crain Communications.

Property and Liability Insurance, 3rd edition. S.S. Huebner and Kenneth Black. Englewood Cliffs, New Jersey: Prentice Hall, Incorporated, 1982.

Reinsurance Directory. Wingdale, New York: Strain Publishing, Incorporated.

Source Book of Health Insurance Data. Washington, D.C.: Health Insurance Association of America, Public Relations Division.

Sources issue of Life Insurance Selling. St. Louis, Missouri: Commerce Publishing Company.

Statistics of Fraternal Benefit Societies. Naperville, Illinois: National Fraternal Congress of America.

The Actuary. (weekly) Chicago, Illinois: Society of Actuaries.

The Insurance Forum. (monthly) Ellettsville, Indiana: Insurance Forum, Incorporated.

The Insurance Legislative Fact Book & Almanac. Brookfield, Wisconsin: Conference of Insurance Legislators.

Underwriting in Life and Health Insurance. Richard Bailey. Roswell, Georgia: Professional Book Distributors, 1985.

Who's Who in Insurance. Englewood, New Jersey: Underwriter Printing & Publishing Company.

Who Writes What in Life and Health Insurance. Cincinnati, Ohio: National Underwriter Company.

World Insurance Directory. Chicago, Illinois: Longman Financial Services.

Appendix E

External
Data Base Sources

Nexis, Newsnet
and Dialog

NEXIS

Newspaper Files
American Banker
BBC Summary of World Broadcasts and Monitoring Reports
The Bond Buyer
The Current Digest of the Soviet Press
Computerworld
The Christian Science Monitor
DM News
Facts on File World News Digest
Financial Times
InfoWorld
The Japan Economic Journal
Los Angeles Times
Legal Times
The MacNeil/Lehrer NewsHour
Manchester Guardian Weekly
The National Law Journal
The New York Times
The Washington Post

Magazine Files
ABA Banking Journal
ADWEEK
Aerospace America

Aviation Week & Space Technology
The Magazine of Bank Administration
Issues in Bank Regulation
Journal of Bank Research
Business Week
BYTE
Chemical Engineering
Chemical Week
Coal Age
Congressional Quarterly Weekly Report
Data Communications
Defense Electronics
Defense and Foreign Affairs
Discover
Dun's Business Month
The Economist
Electronics
Engineering and Mining Journal
Engineering News-Record
Congressional Quarterly Editorial Research Reports
Financial World
Foreign Affairs
Forbes
Fortune
Harvard Business Review
High Technology
International Defense Review
Interavia Aerospace Review
Inc.
Industry Week
Life
Maclean's
Mechanical Engineering
Marine Engineering/Log
Microwave Systems News & Communications Technology
Mining Journal
Mining Magazine
Mining Annual Review
Money
National Journal
Nuclear News

Newsweek
Offshore
Oil & Gas Journal
People
Public Relations Journal
Sports Illustrated
Time
United States Banker
U.S. News & World Report
The Washington Quarterly

Wire Files

The Associated Press world, national, business and sports
 wires
Asahi News Service
Business Wire
Central News Agency
Reuters North European News Service
The Inter Press Service
Jiji Press Ticker Service
Kyodo English Language News Service
PR Newswire
Reuters General News Report
States News Service
Southwest Newswire
United Press International world, national, business and sports
 wires
United Press International State and Regional Wires through
 12-31-85
United Press International State and Regional Wires beginning
 1-1-86
Xinhua (New China) News Agency

Newsletter Files

Ad Day
Advanced Manufacturing Technology
Interavia Air Letter
Advanced Military Computing
Update/The American States
Bioprocessing Technology
McGraw-Hill's Biotechnology Newswatch
Banking Expansion Reporter

Corporate EFT Report
Coal Week International
Coal Outlook
Coal Week
Communications Daily
Coal & Synfuels Technology
ChemWeek Newswire
Defense Industry Report
Defense & Foreign Affairs Daily
Defense & Foreign Affairs Weekly
Daily Report for Executives
East Asian Executive Reports
EFT Report
Electrical Marketing
Electric Utility Week
E&MJ Mining Activity Digest
Enhanced Recovery Week
The Executive Speaker
The Expert and the Law
FEDWATCH
Foster Natural Gas Report
Financial Services Week
Genetic Technology News
Green Markets
Health Care Financing
High-Tech MATERIALS Alert
Inside Energy/with Federal Lands
Inside F.E.R.C.
Inside N.R.C.
Inside R&D
Keystone News Bulletin
Latin American Newsletters
Middle East Executive Reports
Metals Week
Military Space
Morgan Economic Quarterly
NuclearFuel
Nucleonics Week
International Petrochemical Report
Platt's Oligram News
Platt's Oligram Price Report

Securities Week
Space Business News
The Spang Robinson Report
Clean-Coal/Synfuels Letter
Washington Financial Reports
Wharton Economic News Perspectives
World Financial Markets

Business File
Ad Day
ADWEEK
Business Week
Business Wire
DM News
Dun's Business Month
East Asian Executive Reports
The Economist
Engineering News-Record
The Executive Speaker
Financial Times
Forbes
Fortune
Harvard Business Review
Inc.
Industry Week
The Japan Economic Journal
Middle East Executive Reports
Public Relations Journal
PR Newswire
Southwest Newswire

Finance File
ABA Banking Journal
American Banker
The Bond Buyer
The Magazine of Bank Administration
Banking Expansion Reporter
Issues in Bank Regulation
Journal of Bank Research
Corporate EFT Report
EFT Report
FEDWATCH

Financial World
Financial Services Week
Health Care Financing
Money
Morgan Economic Quarterly
Securities Week
United States Banker
Wharton Economic News Perspectives
World Financial Markets

Government File
Congressional Quarterly Weekly Report
Defense & Foreign Affairs
Defense & Foreign Affairs Daily
Defense & Foreign Affairs Weekly
Daily Report for Executives
The Expert and the Law
Foreign Affairs
Legal Times
The National Law Journal
National Journal
States News Service
Washington Financial Reports
The Washington Quarterly

News File
Update/The American States
The Associated Press world, national, business and sports wires
Asahi News Service
BBC Summary of World Broadcasts and Monitoring Reports
The Current Digest of the Soviet Press
Central News Agency
The Christian Science Monitor
Congressional Quarterly Editorial Research Reports
Reuters North European News Service
Facts on File World News Digest
The Inter Press Service
Jiji Press Ticker Service
Kyodo English Language News Service
Latin American Newsletters
Los Angeles Times

Life
The MacNeil/Lehrer NewsHour
Manchester Guardian Weekly
Maclean's
Newsweek
The New York Times
People
Reuters General News Report
Sports Illustrated
Time
United Press International world, national, business and sports wires
United Press International State and Regional Wires beginning 1/1/86
U.S. News & World Report
WorldPaper
The Washington Post
Xinhua(New China)News Agency

Trade/Technology File
Advanced Manufacturing Technology
Aerospace America
Interavia Air Letter
Advanced Military Computing
Aviation Week & Space Technology
Bioprocessing Technology
McGraw-Hill's Biotechnology Newswatch
BYTE
Chemical Engineering
Chemical Week
Computerworld
Coal Age
Coal Week International
Coal Outlook
Coal Week
Communications Daily
Coal & Synfuels Technology
ChemWeek Newswire
Data Communications
Defense Electronics
Defense Industry Report

Discover
Electronics
Electrical Marketing
Electric Utility Week
Engineering and Mining Journal
E&MJ Mining Activity Digest
Enhanced Recovery Week
Foster Natural Gas Report
Genetic Technology News
Green Markets
High Technology
High-Tech MATERIALS Alert
International Defense Review
Interavia Aerospace Review
Inside Energy/with Federal Lands
Inside F.E.R.C.
InfoWorld
Inside N.R.C.
Inside R&D
Keystone News Bulletin
Mechanical Engineering
Marine Engineering/Log
Metals Week
Microwave Systems News & Communications Technology
Military Space
Mining Journal
Mining Magazine
Mining Annual Review
NuclearFuel
Nuclear News
Nucleonics Week
Offshore
Oil & Gas Journal
International Petrochemical Report
Platt's Oilgram News
Platt's Oilgram Price Report
Space Business News
The Spang Robinson Report
Clean-Coal/Synfuels Letter

Magazine ASAP II Files
AFL-CIO News
Aging
American Education
American Heritage
American Libraries
A +
The Atlantic
Backpacker
Boating
Boy's Life
Business America
Canadian America
Car and Driver
Changing Times
Children Today
Creative Computing
Cycle
Datamation
Whole Earth Review
FDA Consumer
Forecast for Home Economics
Flower and Garden
Flying
Food & Nutrition
Golf
Guns & Ammo
Health
High Fidelity
Hot Rod
Journal of Small Business Management
Ladies Home Journal
Monthly Labor Review
Modern Bride
Modern Photography
Motor Trend
Monthly Review
The Nation
NEA Today
The New Leader
The New Republic

Nation's Business
National Review
Natural History
Occupational Outlook Quarterly
Office Administration and Automation
Outdoor Life
PC
PC Week
Peterson's Photographic Magazine
Playboy
Popular Photography
Popular Science
Psychology Today
Your Public Lands
Research & Development
Rolling Stone
Science 83'
Science 84'
Science 85'
Scientific American
Scholastic Choices
Scholastic Update
Scouting
Saturday Evening Post
Skiing
Skin Diver
Sales & Marketing Management
Smithsonian
Sport
Stereo Review
Sunset
Technology Review
Teen
UN Chronicle
UNESCO Courier
World Health
Workbench
The Workbasket and Home Arts Magazine
Washington Monthly
Working Woman
Yachting

Trade & Industry ASAP II Files

AFL-CIO News
Air Transport World
American Metal Market
A+
Automotive Industries
Automotive Marketing
Backstage
Boating Industry
Broadcasting
Best's Review-Life-Health Insurance Edition
Best's Review-Property-Casualty Insurance Edition
Business America
Business & Commercial Aviation
Business History Review
Canadian Business
Computer Decisions
Computer Pictures
Communications News
Consumer Electronics
Construction Review
Creative Computing
Chain Store Age, Executive Edition
Chain Store Age, General Merchandising Edition
Chain Store Age Supermarkets
Gifts & Decorative Accessories
Daily News Record
Drug & Cosmetic Industry
Drug Topics
Discount Store News
Distribution
Electronic Design
Electronic News
Energy User News
Folio: The Magazine for Magazine Management
Foundry Management & Technology
Quick Frozen Foods
Footwear News
Footwear News Magazine
Lawn & Garden Marketing
Government Product News

Graphic Arts Monthly
HFD-The Weekly Home Furnishings Newspaper
Highway & Heavy Construction
Home & Auto
Hospitals, Journal of American Hospital Association
Hardware Age
Handling & Shipping Management
Housewares
Hydraulics & Pneumatics
Implement & Tractor
Institutional Distribution
Infosystems
Interior Design
Iron Age
Jewelers Circular Keystone
Journal of Small Business Management
Federal Home Loan Bank Board Journal
Lodging Hospitality
Machine Design
Medical Laboratory Observer
Meetings & Conventions
Merchandising
Monthly Labor Review
Marketing & Media Decisions
Modern Office Technology
Modern Tire Dealer
Motor Age
Monthly Review
NEA Today
The New Republic
Nursing Homes
Nation's Business
Nation's Restaurant News Newspaper
Occupational Outlook Quarterly
Office Administration and Automation
PC
PC Week
National Petroleum News
Pets-Supplies-Marketing
Plant Engineering
Playthings

Production Engineering
Progressive Architecture
Progressive Grocer
Patient Care
Research & Development
RN
Restaurant Business
School Product News
Skiing Trade News
Sales & Marketing Management
Soap-Cosmetic-Chemical Specialties
Survey of Current Business
Social Security Bulletin
Supermarket Business
Supermarket News
Technology Review
Telephone Engineer & Management
Tooling & Production
Travel Weekly
Ward's Auto World
Women's Wear Daily
Working Women

Encyclopedia Britannica Library Files
Encyclopedia Britannica Micropaedia
Encyclopedia Britannica Macropaedia
Encyclopedia Britannica Book of the Year
Encyclopedia Britannica Medical and Health Annual
Encyclopedia Britannica Science and the Future
Combined File of all Yearbook Documents
Combined File of all Britannica Documents

Government Documents Library Files

Federal Register
Code of Federal Regulations
1981 Code of Federal Regulations
1982 Code of Federal Regulations
1983 Code of Federal Regulations
1984 Code of Federal Regulations
1985 Code of Federal Regulations
Federal Reserve Bulletin

Presidential Documents
Department of State Bulletin
Combined FEDREG & CFR Files

The Information Bank Library Files
Complete Stories from The New York Times
Abstracts of stories selected from newspapers, magazines and
    journals
Advertising and Marketing Intelligence abstracts from selected
    trade and professional publications
Content list of ABS and AMI files
Combined file of ABS and AMI

U.S. Patent and Trademark Office Library Files
Utility patents
Plant patents
Design patents
Patent numbers with classifications
Manual of Classification
Index to Manual of Classification
Combined UTIL, PLANT & DESIGN Files

NEWSNET

Advertising and Marketing
Marketing Research Review
U.S. Employment Opp's—Advertising P/R

Aerospace
Defense Industry Report
Defense R&D Update
Japanese Aviation News: Wing
Satellite Week
Space Calendar
Space Commerce Bulletin
Space Daily
Star Wars Intelligence Report

Automotive
Electric Vehicle Progress
Runzheimer on Automotive Alternatives

Building and Construction
Engelsman's Construction Cost Indexes
Manufactured Housing Newsletter

Chemical
Hazardous Waste News
Sludge Newsletter
State Regulation Report: Toxics
Toxic Materials News
Toxic Materials Transport

Corporate Communications
Sid Cato's Newsletter on Annual Reports

Education
College Press Service

Electronics and Computers
Bulletin Board Systems
Business Computer, The
Computer Book Review
Computer Cookbook, The
Computer Market Observer
Computing Today!
Consumer Electronics
Data Base Informer
HR/PC Online
IDB Online—The Computing Industry Daily
Japan Computer Industry Scan
Japan High Tech Review
Japan Semiconductor Quarterly
Microcomputers in Education
Mini/Micro Bulletin
NASA Software Directory
Optical Information Systems Update
Outlook on IBM
Personal Computers Today
Report on IBM, The
Robotronics Age Newsletter
S. Klein Newsletter on Computer Graphics
Semiconductor Industry & Business Survey
Seybold Report on Professional Computing
Software in Print

Spang Robinson Report on AI
Stewart Alsop's P.C. Letter
Telecommuting Report
U.S. Employment Opp's—The Computer Field

Energy
Daily Petro Futures
Solar Energy Intelligence Report
Utility Reporter—Fuels, Energy & Power

Entertainment and Leisure
Fearless Taster
The Gold Sheet
The Hollywood Hotline
Sports Industry News
Video Week

Environment
Air/Water Pollution Report
Environment Compliance Update
Land Use Planning Report
Nuclear Waste News
World Environment

Farming and Food
Washington Beverage Insight
World Food & Drink Report

Finance and Accounting
American Banker
Banking Regulator
Consumer Credit Letter
Corporate EFT Report
Credit Market Analysis
Credit Unit Regulator
EFT Report
Financial Services Week
Forex Commentary
Forex Watch
U.S. Employment Opp's—Banking/Finance

General Business
BNA Executive Day
Business Currents

Consumers Union News Digest
German Business Scope
German Business Weekly
IBC Barter Countertrade—Haves
IBC Barter Countertrade—Wants
IBC Bids and Buyers Clearinghouse
IBC Inventory Liquidation Clearinghouse
IBC Sellers Clearinghouse
McGraw-Hill Seminars & Business Info
Sales Prospector/CA AZ NV HI
Sales Prospector/CO ID MT OR UT WA WY AK
Sales Prospector/Canada
Sales Prospector/GA FL AL NC SC
Sales Prospector/IL IN
Sales Prospector/LA MS AR OK KY TN
Sales Prospector/MD VA WV NC SC DC
Sales Prospector/MO KS IA NB
Sales Prospector/NY NJ Southern CT
Sales Prospector/New England
Sales Prospector/OH MI
Sales Prospector/Ohio River Valley
Sales Prospector/PA DE Southern NJ
Sales Prospector/TX OK NM
Sales Prospector/WI MN IA ND SD

Government
Access Reports/Freedom of Information
BNA Congressional/Presidential Calendar
BNA's Daily Report for Executives
Congressional Activities
Defense Week
FTC FOIA Log
FTC: Watch
Information Report, The
Navy News & Undersea Technology
PACs & Lobbies
Surplus Alert
U.S. Census Report
U.S. Employment Opp's—Federal Gov't

Health and Hospital
Biomedical Safety and Standards

Diack Newsletter
Health Cost Management Weekly
MMWR
Plus Prescription Drug Update

Insurance
IMS Weekly Marketeer

International
APS Diplomat
Africa News
Asia Cable
Asian Intelligence
Central America Update
China Express Contracts
Exporter, The
Frost & Sullivan's Political Risk Letter
High Tech International
International Travel Warning Service
Japan Technology Bulletin
Japan Weekly Monitor
Latin American Debt Chronicle
Mid-East Business Digest
NPD Mexico Daily News Briefs
Tax Notes International
World Business Asia—Pacific Weekly
World Business Intelligence Daily
World Business Latin America Weekly
World Business Middle East Weekly
World Business Sub-Sahara Africa Weekly
World Business Western Europe Weekly

Investment
Aps Review
Biotechnology Investment Opportunities
Boot Cove Economic Forecast
Daily Industrial Index Analyzer
Financial Focus
Ford Investment Review
Futures Focus
Futures Focus Stock Index Plus
Insider Trading News Daily
International BusinessMan News Report

Investext/Aerospace
Investext/Automotive
Investext/Broadcasting—Cable TV
Investext/Building Materials
Investext/Chemicals
Investext/Computers and Office Equipment
Investext/Data Processing
Investext/Electrical and Electronics
Investext/Financial
Investext/Food Processing
Investext/Food and Lodging
Investext/Health Care
Investext/Natural Resources
Investext/Oil & Gas Services and Equipment
Investext/Pharmaceuticals
Investext/Printing and Publishing
Investext/Real Estate and Construction
Investext/Retailing
Investext/Scientific & Tech Instruments
Investext/Telecommunications
Investext/Utilities
Michael Linden's Free Market Digest
Mutual Fund Monitor
NASDAQ
Newswire Daily
OTC Onsight
Ober Income Letter Profit Report
Silicon Mountain Report
Stanger Report, The
Trendvest Ratings
Wall St. Monitor:Weekly Market Digest
Wall Street S.O.S
Wellington's Capital
Wellington's Letter
Wellington's Letter Tradeline
Wellington's Tradeline Bulletin Service

Law
Industrial Health & Hazards Update
Lawyer's Micro Users Group Newsletter
Reports of Interest to Lawyers

Management
Service Dealer's Newsletter

Manufacturing
Computerized Manufacturing

Medicine
Biomedical Technology Info Service
Biotech Update
Clinical Lab Letter
Medical Abstracts Newsletter
Radiology & Imaging
U.S. Medical Research Update

Metals and Mining
Daily Metals Report
Iron & Steel Technology Insights

Office
Seybold Report on Office Systems, The

Public Relations
PR Hi-Tech Alert/Video Monitor
PR Newswire

Publishing and Broadcasting
CD Data Report
Copyright Management
Editors Only
Electronic Information Report
IIA Friday Memo
Kirkus Book Reviews
MicroPublishing Report
NA Hotline
NewsNet Action Letter
NewsNet's Online Bulletin
PhotoBulletin
PhotoMarket
Photo Letter, The
Public Broadcasting Report
Seybold Report on Publishing Systems, The
Television Digest
Travelwriter Marketletter
Viewdata/Videotex Report

Wiley Book News
Worldwide Videotex Update

Real Estate
Real Estate & Venture Funding Directory
Real Estate Buyers Directory

Research & Development
American Bulletin of Technology Transfer
Engineering Microsoftware Review
Federal Research Report
Innovator's Digest
Invention Management

Social Sciences
ChurchNews International
RFC News Service
RNS Daily News Reports
United Methodist Information

Taxation
BNA Tax Updates
BNA's Daily Tax Report
BNA's Private Letter Rulings Report
CCH Tax Day:Federal
CCH Tax Day:State
Charitable Giving Techniques
Small Business Tax Review, The
Tax Directory, The
Tax Management Weekly
Tax Notes Today

Telecommunications
BOC Week
Cable & Satellite Express News
Cambron's BBS Directory
Common Carrier Week
Communications Daily
DBS News
Data Channels
Digital Bypass Report
FCC Daily Digest
FCC Week

Fiber Optics News
ISIS New Electronic Media Newswire
ISIS Private Videotex System Database
ISIS Public Access System Database
Industrial Communications
Interconnection
International Communications Week
International Videotex Teletext News
Long-Distance Letter, The
Mobile Phone News
NTT Topics
Public Access Videotex Directory
Report on AT&T
Satellite News
Satellite Television Newsletter
State Telephone Regulation Report
Telecommunications Counselor
Telecommunications Reports
Telephone News
Tenant Communications
Videotex Now Newswire
Videotex Products
Viewtext
Wiretap

Tobacco
TMA Bits
TMA Cigarettes and Cigars
TMA Executive Summary
TMA International Executive Summary
TMA Issues Monitor
TMA Leaf Bulletin Summary
TMA National Bulletin
TMA Smoking:Chewing and Snuff
TMA State Bulletin

Transportation and Shipping
Public Transit Report
Reistrup Report:Rail & Intermodal
U.S. Rail News

Travel and Tourism
Business Hotel & Meeting Site Reviews
Business Traveler's Letter

United Press International
UPI Business & Financial Wire
UPI Domestic News Wire
UPI International News Wire
UPI Political Wire
UPI Sports Wire

USA Today Update
USA Today Decisionline/Banking & Economy
USA Today Decisionline/Business Law
USA Today Decisionline/Energy
USA Today Decisionline/Insurance
USA Today Decisionline/Issues & Debates
USA Today Decisionline/Real Estate
USA Today Decisionline/Technology
USA Today Decisionline/Telecommunication
USA Today Decisionline/Travel
USA Today Decisionline/Trends/Marketing
USA Today Hotline/International
USA Today Hotline/Money
USA Today Hotline/News
USA Today Hotline/Weather
USA Today Index News Bulletin
USA Today Special Reports

Dialog

Agriculture And Nutrition:
Agricola 79-present
Agricola 70-78
Biosis Previews 81-present
Biosis Previews 77-80
Biosis Previews 69-76
Cab Abstracts
CRIS/USDA
Food Science & Technology Abstracts
Foods Adlibra

Bibliography—Books And Monographs:
Book Review Index
Books In Print
Dialog Publications
GPO Monthly Catalog
GPO Publications Reference File
LC Marc
Remarc pre-1900 and n.d.
Remarc 1900-1939
Remarc 1940-1959
Remarc 1960-1969
Remarc 1970-end
Wiley Catalog/online

Business/Economics:

Textual
ABI/inform
Adtrack
Arthur D. Little/online
Biobusiness
Chemical Industry Notes
Coffeeline
Economic Literature Index
Find/SVP Reports & Studies Index
Finis: Financial Industry Information Service
Foods Adlibra
Foreign Trade & Econ Abstracts
Harvard Business Review
Industry Data Sources
Insurance Abstracts
Investext
Management Contents
Media General Databank
Pharmaceutical News Index
PTS Annual Reports Abstracts
PTS Defense Markets & Technology
PTS F & S Indexes 72-78
PTS F & S Indexes 79-present
PTS Marketing & Advertising Reference Service
PTS Promt
Standard & Poor's Corporate Descriptions

Standard & Poor's News
Trade & Industry ASAP
Trade & Industry Index

Numeric
BLS Consumer Price Index
BLS Employment, Hours, and Earnings
BLS Producer Price Index
Cendata
Disclosure II
Donnelley Demographics
PTS International Forecasts
PTS International Time Series
PTS U.S. Forecasts
PTS U.S. Time Series
U.S. Exports

Directories
Business Software Database
Commerce Business Daily
Commerce Business Daily 9/82-current month
Compare Products
D&B—Dun's Market Identifiers
D&B—International Dun's Market Identifiers
D&B—Million Dollar Directory
Disclosure II
Disclosure/Spectrum Ownership
Electronic Yellow Pages Index
Electronic Yellow Pages Index—Construction
Electronic Yellow Pages Index—Financial Services
Electronic Yellow Pages Index—Manufacturers
Electronic Yellow Pages Index—Professionals
Electronic Yellow Pages Index—Retailers 5200-5499
Electronic Yellow Pages Index—Retailers 5500-5799
Electronic Yellow Pages Index—Retailers 5800-5999
Electronic Yellow Pages Index—Services 7000-7299
Electronic Yellow Pages Index—Services 7300-7999
Electronic Yellow Pages Index—Wholesalers
Foreign Traders Index
ICC British Company Directory
ICC British Company Financial Datasheets
International Listing Service

Moody's Corporate News—International
Moody's Corporate News—U.S.
Moody's Corporate Profiles
OAG Electronic Edition
Standard & Poor's Register—Biographical
Standard & Poor's Register—Corporate
Thomas Register Online
Trade Opportunities
Trade Opportunities Weekly
Trinet Company Database
Trinet Establishment Database

Chemistry:
CA Search 67-71
CA Search 72-76
CA Search 77-79
CA Search 80-81
CA Search 82-present
Chemical Exposure
Chemical Industry Notes
Chemical Regulations and Guidelines System
Chemname
Chemsearch
Chemsis 67-71
Chemsis 72-76
Chemsis 77-81
Chemsis 82-present
Chemzero
Claims Compound Registry
Paperchem
Scisearch 74-77
Scisearch 78-80
Scisearch 81-83
Scisearch 84-present
TSCA Initial Inventory

Current Affairs:
AP News Daily
AP News 7/84-present
Canadian Business & Current Affairs
Chronolog
Facts On File

Magazine ASAP
Magazine Index
National Newspaper Index
Newsearch
Online Chronicle
PAIS International
Standard & Poor's News
UPI News Daily
UPI News 4/83-current month
World Affairs Report

Directories:
American Men & Women Of Science
Biography Master Index A-M
Biography Master Index N-Z
Career Placement Registry/Experienced
Career Placement Registry/Student
Database Of Databases
Encyclopedia Of Associations
Marquis Pro-files
Marquis Who's Who
Ulrich's International Periodicals Directory

Education:
AIM/ARM
A-V Online
Electronic Directory Of Education
Eric
Exceptional Child Education Resources
NICSEM/NIMIS
Peterson's College Database

Energy And Environment:
Aptic Aquaculture
Aqualine
Aquatic Sciences & Fisheries Abstracts
Biosis Previews 81-present
Biosis Previews 77-80
Biosis Previews 69-76
CA Search 67-71
CA Search 72-76
CA Search 77-79

CA Search 80-81
CA Search 82-present
Doe Energy 83-present
Doe Energy 74-82
Electric Power Database
Energyline
Energynet
Enviroline
Environmental Bibliography
Oceanic Abstracts
P/E News
Pollution Abstracts
Water Resources Abstracts
Waternet

Foundations And Grants:
Foundation Directory
Foundation Grants Index
Grants
National Foundations

Law And Government:
ASI
Chemical Regulations & Guidelines System
CIS
Commerce Business Daily (daily)
Commerce Business Daily 9/82-current month
Congressional Record Abstracts
Criminal Justice Periodical Index
Federal Index
Federal Register Abstracts
GPO Monthly Catalog
GPO Publications Reference File
IRS Taxinfo
Laborlaw
Legal Resource Index
NCJRS
NTIS
Patlaw
TCSA Initial Inventory

Materials Sciences:
CA Search 67-71
CA Search 72-76
CA Search 77-79
CA Search 80-81
CA Search 82-present
Chemname
Chemsearch
Chemsis 67-71
Chemsis 72-76
Chemsis 77-81
Chemsis 82-present
Chemzero
Metadex
Nonferrous Metals Abstracts
Paperchem
Textile Technology Abstracts
World Aluminum Abstracts
World Textiles

Medicine And Biosciences:
Biobusiness
Biosis Previews 81-present
Biosis Previews 77-80
Biosis Previews 69-76
CA Search 67-71
CA Search 72-76
CA Search 77-79
CA Search 80-81
CA Search 82-present
Chemname
Chemsearch
Chemsis 67-71
Chemsis 72-76
Chemsis 77-81
Chemsis 82-present
Chemzero
Drug Information Fulltext
Embase 74-79
Embase 80-81
Embase 82-present

Embase in process
Health Planning & Administration
International Pharmaceutical Abstracts
Life Science Collection
Medline 66-72
Medline 73-79
Medline 80-present
Mental Health Abstracts
Nursing & Allied Health
Occupational Safety And Health
Pharmaceutical News Index
Scisearch 74-77
Scisearch 78-80
Scisearch 81-83
Scisearch 84-present
Telegen
Zoological Record

Multidisciplinary:
Academic American Encyclopedia
Conference Papers Index
Dialindex
Dissertation Abstracts Online
Everyman's Encyclopedia
Federal Research In Progress Abridged
Federal Research In Progress Unabridged
NTIS

Online Training And Practice:
Ontap ABI/inform
Ontap Biosis Previews
Ontap CA Search
Ontap Cab Abstracts
Ontap Chemname
Ontap Compendex
Ontap Dialindex
Ontap Eric
Ontap Inspec
Ontap Magazine Index
Ontap Medline
Ontap PTS Promt
Ontap Scisearch

Ontap Social Scisearch
Ontap Trademarkscan
Ontap World Patents Index

Patents And Trademarks:
CA Search 67-71
CA Search 72-76
CA Search 77-79
CA Search 80-81
CA Search 82-present
Claims/Citation pre-47
Claims/Citation 47-70
Claims/Citation 71-present
Claims/Class
Claims Compound Registry
Claims/Reassignment & Reexamination
Claims/U.S. Patents 50-70
Claims/U.S. Patent Abstracts 71-81
Claims/U.S. Patent Abstracts 82-present
Claims/U.S. Patent Abstracts Weekly
Claims/Uniterm 50-70
Claims/Uniterm 71-81
Claims/Uniterm 82-present
Patlaw
Trademarkscan
World Patents Index 63-80
World Patents Index Latest 81-present

Science And Technology:
Aerospace Database
Business Software Database
Computer Database
Ei Engineering Meetings
Federal Research In Progress abridged
Federal Research In Progress unabridged
Fluidex
Geoarchive
Georef
Inspec 69-77
Inspec 78-present
ISMEC
Mathfile

Menu—International Software Database
Meteorological & Geoastrophysical Abstracts
Microcomputer Index
NTIS
Scisearch 74-77
Scisearch 78-80
Scisearch 81-83
Scisearch 84-present
Soviet Science And Technology
Spin
Ssie Current Research
Standards & Specifications
Tris
Weldasearch

Social Sciences And Humanities:
America: History & Life
Artbibliographies Modern
Child Abuse And Neglect
Family Resources
Historical Abstracts
Information Science Abstracts
Language & Language Behavior Abstracts
Lisa
Middle East: Abstracts & Index
Mideast File
MLA Bibliography
PAIS International
Philosopher's Index
Population Bibliography
PsycAlert
PsycInfo
Religion Index
Rila
Rilm Abstracts
Social Scisearch
Sociological Abstracts
U.S. Political Science Abstracts
World Affairs Report

Appendix F

Interview Guide

POTENTIAL SOURCES

Intelligence Questions	Sales	Marketing	Finance	R & D	Production	Facilities	Personnel	Planning	Legal	Purchasing	Senior Management	Data Processing
Purchasing												
Who are the top five suppliers of major raw materials, by dollars and/or by units?		X	X		X					X		X
Have there been any changes in suppliers of principal raw materials in the past two years, If so, why?	X	X			X	X				X	X	
Are there single suppliers for major raw materials used by the company?		X	X	X	X					X	X	
What is the duration of outstanding purchasing contracts for major raw materials?			X	X	X			X	X	X	X	
Is there a company wide program to standardize materials and supplies?	X	X	X	X	X			X		X	X	X
Do any materials exhibit unusual inventory turnover, compared to industry averages?			X	X						X		
Is competitive bidding a standard purchasing procedure?			X						X	X	X	

205

POTENTIAL SOURCES

Intelligence Questions	Sales	Marketing	Finance	R & D	Production	Facilities	Personnel	Planning	Legal	Purchasing	Senior Management	Data Processing
Are formal Economic Order Quantity (EOQ) models utilized?												
Sales												
What is their customer mix?	X	X						X			X	X
What is their product mix?	X	X						X			X	X
What is the company's sales volume by dollars and/or units? In total? By product/service group?	X	X	X	X	X	X	X	X	X	X	X	X
What is the average sales backlog in dollars?	X	X	X					X			X	X
Are sales forecasted based on real assessments of the market or on percentage increases?	X	X	X						X			X
What is the estimated sales volume to the top ten customers in each geographic region?	X	X						X			X	X
What percentage of the company's sales are government contracts?	X	X	X					X	X		X	X
What are the total number of domestic accounts?	X	X	X					X			X	X
How many customers does the company have in major foreign markets?	X	X	X		X			X			X	X
What percentage of total business is attributed to national accounts?	X	X						X			X	X
How much of the total business is list price business?	X	X	X					X			X	X

POTENTIAL SOURCES

Intelligence Questions	Sales	Marketing	Finance	R & D	Production	Facilities	Personnel	Planning	Legal	Purchasing	Senior Management	Data Processing
Where are the regional sales offices located?	X	X	X			X	X	X	X	X	X	X
How many field sales personnel are located in each regional sales office?	X	X					X				X	X
How many sales calls is a sales person expected to make per day?	X	X						X			X	X
What are the sales tools, such as visual aids, special analyses, etc., employed by field sales?	X	X									X	X
What sales training programs are available?	X	X					X				X	
What compensation packages are in place for the field sales force?	X	X	X			X		X	X		X	X
What sales programs have been launched to expand customer base and increase sales with existing customers?	X	X									X	
What factors determine the basis for price quotations?	X	X						X			X	
What are the major sales and service advantages which the company offers its customers?	X	X						X			X	
Is timely delivery an important sales advantage?	X	X			X						X	
Is the relationship between the company and its distributors improving or deteriorating?	X	X									X	

POTENTIAL SOURCES

Intelligence Questions	Sales	Marketing	Finance	R & D	Production	Facilities	Personnel	Planning	Legal	Purchasing	Senior Management	Data Processing
How does the company's policy for distributor margins compare with those of the competition?	X	X	X					X			X	
What types of reports are regularly provided by major distributors to the company?	X	X						X			X	
What has been the recent history in stockouts, substitutes and backorders?	X	X			X			X		X	X	X
What is the rate of new account acquisition?	X	X						X			X	X
Has the company identified a trend among major customers which would account for any loss of business?	X	X						X			X	
What is the recent trend in average account size?	X	X	X					X	X		X	
Research and Development												
What is the background of the Director of Research and Development?				X			X				X	
What is the overall caliber of the research staff?				X				X			X	
How is the R & D effort organized—by division, product, group or market? Is there a centralized R & D structure?	X	X	X	X	X	X	X	X		X	X	X
Where are the research and development laboratories located?				X				X			X	
What are the major sources of the funding for R & D?					X	X		X			X	

POTENTIAL SOURCES

Intelligence Questions	Sales	Marketing	Finance	R & D	Production	Facilities	Personnel	Planning	Legal	Purchasing	Senior Management	Data Processing
What is the R & D budget? In total? By product?			X	X				X			X	X
What are the current R & D expenditures as a percentage of sales?		X	X					X			X	X
How are R & D projects established?		X		X				X			X	
How do the company's expenditures for research and development compare to the industry average?		X	X	X				X			X	
Where is the major R & D thrust?	X	X		X			X	X			X	
What significant new products are currently under development?	X	X	X	X				X		X	X	X
Within the last five years, what are the significant new products and/or processes resulting from R & D efforts?	X	X	X	X	X	X		X		X	X	
Where is the emphasis placed for the development of new products? (i.e. modify existing lines, products for new markets, products for new customer/industries)	X	X		X				X			X	
What is the company's perceived technical position relative to its competitors?				X				X			X	
What degree of technological intensity exists within the industry?	X	X		X	X			X			X	
Who is the technological leader in the industry?	X	X		X				X			X	

POTENTIAL SOURCES

Intelligence Questions	Sales	Marketing	Finance	R & D	Production	Facilities	Personnel	Planning	Legal	Purchasing	Senior Management	Data Processing
How crucial are patents? Is the company's patent position strong in any particular product line?		X		X				X			X	
Legal												
Are any company officers or directors involved in criminal or civil litigation?		X	X				X	X	X		X	
Is the company involved in any product liability suits?	X	X	X	X	X			X	X		X	
Are there any major legal disputes with customers, subcontractors or suppliers?	X	X	X	X	X	X	X	X	X	X	X	X
Is the company involved in any antitrust litigation?		X	X				X	X		X		
Are there any formal charges pending before federal or state labor agencies?			X				X		X		X	
How have federal or state labor charges been resolved in the past?			X				X				X	
Is the company's patent and trademark protection policy sound or weak?		X		X				X	X		X	
What significant patents or trademarks does the company hold?	X	X		X				X	X		X	
Planning												
What is the basic approach to tactical and strategic planning?	X							X			X	
What is the company's growth strategy over the next five years?	X	X						X			X	

POTENTIAL SOURCES

Intelligence Questions	Sales	Marketing	Finance	R & D	Production	Facilities	Personnel	Planning	Legal	Purchasing	Senior Management	Data Processing
What are the company's areas of greatest emphasis?	X	X						X			X	
What key goals are monitored on an ongoing basis?		X						X			X	
Is it more likely that the company will grow by acquisition, penetration of new markets or by increased market share in existing markets?	X	X						X			X	
Is the company engaged in the development of new products, technology or markets?	X	X		X	X			X			X	
Do long range plans include alternative strategies for competitor reactions?								X			X	
What are the potential revenues and expenses of each alternative business strategy? What are the manpower and capital requirements of each alternative?			X					X			X	
What position is in charge of long range planning, who holds the position and what is his or her title?	X	X		X			X	X			X	
To what extent are documented objectives used in planning?		X						X			X	
What methods are used to monitor customer needs and competitor strategies?	X	X						X			X	
How well does the company forecast its demand?			X						X			X

POTENTIAL SOURCES

Intelligence Questions	Sales	Marketing	Finance	R & D	Production	Facilities	Personnel	Planning	Legal	Purchasing	Senior Management	Data Processing
How does the company's organizational structure affect its overall goal?								X			X	
Pricing												
What are their prices for specific products or services?	X	X	X		X						X	X
How would you characterize the pricing policy of the company?	X	X	X		X						X	
What is the three year price history of the most significant product sold by the company?	X	X	X		X						X	X
In which of the major markets does the company consider itself to be a pricing leader?	X	X	X		X						X	
What types of discounts do they offer: cash, quantity and/or seasonal?	X	X	X		X						X	X
What special discounts are offered to top customers?	X	X	X		X						X	X
How does the company's discount structure compare to that of its competitors?	X	X	X		X						X	
How has the company passed along cost increases to the customer in the form of pricing?	X	X	X		X						X	
What are the trends in credit policies?	X	X	X		X						X	

POTENTIAL SOURCES

Intelligence Questions	Sales	Marketing	Finance	R & D	Production	Facilities	Personnel	Planning	Legal	Purchasing	Senior Management	Data Processing
Distribution												
What is the nature of the company's distribution channels?	X	X					X	X		X		
What percentage of total sales moves through each distribution channel?	X	X					X			X		
What primary means of transportation are employed to reach major markets?	X	X	X		X	X	X			X	X	
What are distribution costs as a percentage of net sales?		X	X				X			X	X	
Have there been significant changes in the way the company distributes its products in major markets?	X	X	X				X			X		
Are there any plans for significant changes in the way the company distributes its products?		X					X	X		X		
Data Processing												
How sophisticated is the electronic data processing capability of the company?	X	X	X		X	X	X			X	X	
Is the electronic data processing function centralized?						X					X	X
To what extent are local and regional sales offices computerized?	X	X				X				X	X	X

POTENTIAL SOURCES

Intelligence Questions	Sales	Marketing	Finance	R & D	Production	Facilities	Personnel	Planning	Legal	Purchasing	Senior Management	Data Processing
Facilities												
How many facilities does the company own, where are they located and what type of facility is it?	X	X	X	X	X	X	X	X	X	X	X	X
How much space is attributed to office and plant?			X	X	X	X	X	X		X	X	X
What is the capacity and utilization of each factory?		X			X	X		X			X	
What type of space is available for expansion?		X			X	X		X			X	
Does the company have any idle plants or excess facilities?	X	X	X		X	X		X			X	
Does the company have any leases on plant or equipment that are near expiration?			X		X	X		X		X	X	X
What is the condition of the equipment on lease?			X		X	X		X		X	X	
Is the company actively considering selling any major piece of plant or equipment?			X		X	X		X		X	X	
What is the type of electrical power needed for the manufacturing equipment?					X	X				X		
Where would the company move if it had to?	X	X	X		X	X		X			X	
Marketing												
What types of products/ services does the company offer?	X	X	X	X	X	X	X	X	X	X	X	X
What is the market share for each of the company's products?	X	X	X	X	X			X			X	X

POTENTIAL SOURCES

Intelligence Questions	Sales	Marketing	Finance	R & D	Production	Facilities	Personnel	Planning	Legal	Purchasing	Senior Management	Data Processing
Who are the major customers?	X	X	X		X			X			X	X
What customers would the company like to attract?	X	X	X	X	X			X			X	
What market segments has the company been successful in?	X	X	X	X	X			X			X	
What market segments provide maximum opportunity for growth?	X	X						X			X	
How do you think the product mix and customer mix will change over the next few years?	X	X		X	X			X			X	
How has the product and customer mix changed over the last five years?	X	X		X	X			X			X	
What is being done to differentiate the product in the market?	X	X		X	X	X		X		X	X	
What is the company's history in finding new uses for existing products?	X	X		X	X			X			X	
What product lines will be added/deleted?	X	X		X	X			X			X	
Does the company have any superior guarantees on its products and/or services?	X	X			X				X		X	X
What are the recent trends in the quality of the products and services in the industry?	X	X		X	X	X		X		X	X	
What do you consider to be the strongest point of your competitive advantage in the industry?	X	X	X	X	X			X			X	

POTENTIAL SOURCES

Intelligence Questions	Sales	Marketing	Finance	R & D	Production	Facilities	Personnel	Planning	Legal	Purchasing	Senior Management	Data Processing
How many competitors does the company have and how large are they?	X	X	X	X	X		X	X	X	X	X	X
Who are the company's current and potential competitors?	X	X	X	X	X		X	X	X	X	X	X
Who are the top three competitors in each major line of business?	X	X		X				X			X	
To what degree is research done on competitor products?	X	X		X				X	X		X	
What competitor weakness could the company capitalize on?	X	X	X	X	X	X	X	X	X	X	X	X
What procedures are used to monitor the marketplace?	X	X		X				X			X	X
How well can the company forecast demand for its products and services?	X	X	X	X	X			X			X	X
What are the primary factors influencing growth of major markets of the industry?	X	X		X	X			X			X	
Are products always researched and test marketed with limited distribution before a national rollout?	X	X		X	X			X			X	
What is management's view toward the sensitivity of market demand to price changes?	X	X	X	X	X			X		X	X	
What is the relationship of the delivery cycle to the manufacturing cycle?	X	X			X						X	
To what extent are finished products standardized?		X		X	X			X			X	

POTENTIAL SOURCES

Intelligence Questions	Sales	Marketing	Finance	R & D	Production	Facilities	Personnel	Planning	Legal	Purchasing	Senior Management	Data Processing
What are their methods of distribution?	X	X		X	X	X		X		X	X	X
How are sales distributed by geographical areas?	X	X			X						X	
How important is the proximity of the plant to customers?	X	X			X	X		X		X	X	
What is the image of the firm in various geographical regions?	X	X			X	X		X		X	X	
What does the company consider as its primary advertising and promotional media?	X	X	X					X			X	X
What is the company's attitude toward private labeling its products?	X	X			X	X		X			X	X
Top Management												
What image is the company attempting to project?	X	X	X			X	X	X			X	
What are the company's major businesses?	X	X	X	X	X	X	X	X	X	X	X	X
What are the company's objectives? Goals? Specific strategies?	X	X	X	X	X	X	X	X	X	X	X	X
What are the names of the subsidiaries and divisions owned by the company?		X	X			X	X	X	X		X	
How autonomous are subsidiaries?		X	X	X	X			X	X	X	X	
If the stock is closely held, who are the principal owners and what percentage of stock is held by each?			X					X	X		X	

POTENTIAL SOURCES

Intelligence Questions	Sales	Marketing	Finance	R & D	Production	Facilities	Personnel	Planning	Legal	Purchasing	Senior Management	Data Processing
What is the organizational structure for all top officers?		X					X	X			X	
What is the name and background of each director and principal officer?							X		X		X	
What is name, title and background of the person who is responsible for long range planning?		X	X	X	X	X	X	X	X		X	
What is the relationship between responsibility and authority for all levels of personnel within the company?	X	X	X	X	X	X	X	X	X	X	X	X
What is the characteristic management style throughout the company?	X	X	X	X	X	X	X	X	X	X	X	X
How are the top three layers of the organization structured?		X	X	X	X		X	X	X	X	X	
Are you aware of any unfilled positions at the director level or above?		X					X	X	X		X	
Does the company formally identify backup candidates for key management positions? Who are they?		X	X	X	X		X	X	X			X
What characteristics are crucial to ascend to top management positions?							X	X			X	
Who are the actual "Movers and Shakers" in the company?	X	X	X	X	X	X	X	X	X	X	X	X
What is the morale of the professional level staff?	X	X	X	X	X	X	X	X	X	X	X	X

POTENTIAL SOURCES

Intelligence Questions	Sales	Marketing	Finance	R & D	Production	Facilities	Personnel	Planning	Legal	Purchasing	Senior Management	Data Processing
Is there any dominate industry from which key personnel are drawn?							X	X	X		X	
Which competitor has attracted the most key personnel from the company in the past two years?		X	X	X	X		X	X	X		X	
Who is responsible for the budgeting process?			X	X	X	X	X	X	X		X	
What are the characteristics of successful companies in the industry?	X	X	X	X	X			X	X		X	
Does the company have any unusual business policies which differ from competition?	X	X	X	X	X		X	X	X	X	X	
How did the company achieve its present position in the industry?		X	X					X	X		X	
How successfully have newly acquired businesses been integrated into the company?								X	X		X	
Are there any environmental obstacles facing the company?		X		X	X			X			X	
How can the company's resources be employed to exploit new business opportunities?		X	X	X				X	X		X	
What is the company's acquisition strategy?			X					X	X		X	
What is the compounded annual growth rate for the organization?	X	X	X					X			X	

POTENTIAL SOURCES

Intelligence Questions	Sales	Marketing	Finance	R & D	Production	Facilities	Personnel	Planning	Legal	Purchasing	Senior Management	Data Processing
Finance												
How strong is the financial management and controllership function?			X				X	X			X	
What type of internal financial reports are issued and how often?	X	X	X	X	X	X	X	X	X	X	X	X
What is the company's overall rate of return? In total? By product line? By business segment?	X	X	X					X			X	
What is the company's return on investment (ROI)?			X					X			X	
What return on investment is adequate?		X	X					X			X	
How does the company compare its returns to other companies within the industry?	X	X	X					X			X	
What is the company's operating revenue?	X	X	X					X	X		X	
What are the company's operating expenses?	X	X	X	X	X	X	X	X	X	X	X	X
What is the company's operating income?	X	X	X					X			X	
What is the company's gross profit by product line?	X	X	X		X			X			X	
What is the company's cash flow?			X					X			X	
What is the trend of each cost element as a ratio to sales?			X					X			X	
What can be learned from other financial ratios?	X	X	X					X			X	

POTENTIAL SOURCES

Intelligence Questions	Sales	Marketing	Finance	R & D	Production	Facilities	Personnel	Planning	Legal	Purchasing	Senior Management	Data Processing
What financial targets does the company consider acceptable and attainable over the planning period?	X	X	X					X			X	
What is the company's current capitalization picture: common stock, preferred stock, long-term debt?			X								X	
What are their best sources for long and short-term capital?			X					X			X	
What capital requirements are needed to sustain long-term growth of "X" percent?		X	X					X			X	
What is the procedure for allocating the capital budget?			X								X	
How are costs (for budgets) estimated and how far down into the company does the budgeting process extend?	X	X	X	X	X	X	X	X	X	X	X	X
What are the major expense categories and relevant significance of each?	X	X	X		X			X			X	X
How will expense control and cash management activities be strengthened?		X	X	X	X						X	
What are the engineering costs for product development, product engineer ing and manufacturing engineering?	X	X	X	X	X			X			X	

POTENTIAL SOURCES

Intelligence Questions	Sales	Marketing	Finance	R & D	Production	Facilities	Personnel	Planning	Legal	Purchasing	Senior Management	Data Processing
What is the relationship of each operation to total product cost?	X	X	X		X						X	X
What is the depreciation policy that is applied to current plant and equipment?			X		X	X					X	X
What economic and financial issues are important to the company?		X	X					X			X	
What is the industry's economic structure and what trends exist?	X	X	X					X			X	
Does the company have unused assets that might be sold?			X		X	X		X		X	X	
Are you aware of any serious offers pending to purchase the company?	X	X	X			X		X	X		X	
What is the appraised value of land for the company?			X			X		X	X		X	X
What are the annual taxes for each facility site?			X		X	X		X	X		X	X
Are there any unusual tax issues in taxation which currently affect operations?			X					X	X		X	
Does the company have significant foreign tax problems or U.S. tax problems relating to its foreign operations?			X					X			X	
Production												
What is the location and size of each manufacturing site?		X	X		X	X		X			X	

POTENTIAL SOURCES

Intelligence Questions	Sales	Marketing	Finance	R & D	Production	Facilities	Personnel	Planning	Legal	Purchasing	Senior Management	Data Processing
Are there plans for the closing of any manufacturing operation and/or sites?		X	X	X	X	X		X	X		X	
What is the maximum capacity for each manufacturing site?		X	X	X	X			X			X	X
What percentage of floor space is used for each manufacturing operation?				X	X			X			X	X
How current is the manufacturing equipment at each plant?					X						X	
What are the major manufacturing operations and their sequence?				X	X			X			X	
What manufacturing processes give the company a competitive edge?	X	X	X	X	X			X			X	
What are the components of production cycle time?				X	X						X	
At what rate is manufacturing productivity increasing or decreasing?				X	X	X			X			X	X
Have any major manufacturing operations been discontinued recently?	X	X	X	X	X	X	X	X	X	X	X	X
Has the company experienced any extraordinary production problems within the last two years?	X	X	X	X	X						X	
Does volume or product mix affect manufacturing time?				X	X						X	
How much production flexibility is available in manufacturing?				X	X						X	

POTENTIAL SOURCES

Intelligence Questions	Sales	Marketing	Finance	R & D	Production	Facilities	Personnel	Planning	Legal	Purchasing	Senior Management	Data Processing
What programs exist for increasing standardization?				X	X						X	
What type of material control procedures exist?			X	X	X					X	X	
Is the company working on new production control processes?				X	X						X	
What is the status of mechanization and automation relative to industry standards?				X	X	X					X	
Is the product design conducive to an efficient manufacturing process?				X	X						X	
Does product design restrict the selection of the manufacturing process?				X	X						X	
What degree of integration exists between product and manufacturing engineering?				X	X						X	
How is the finished goods inventory managed?	X	X			X						X	X
As a percentage of annual sales, how much inventory of finished goods and/or raw material is maintained?			X		X		X				X	X
What are the break-even points for units produced?	X				X						X	
Does the company have any manufacturing cost advantage?	X	X		X	X	X		X		X	X	
What percent of sales is attributed to labor, material and overhead?	X	X	X		X						X	X

POTENTIAL SOURCES

Intelligence Questions	Sales	Marketing	Finance	R & D	Production	Facilities	Personnel	Planning	Legal	Purchasing	Senior Management	Data Processing
What cost improvement programs are underway in manufacturing?			X	X	X						X	
Personnel												
What are the employment and recruiting policies of the company?	X	X	X	X	X	X	X		X	X	X	X
What is the total number of employees by function?	X	X	X	X	X	X	X	X	X	X	X	X
Has the company identified any change in the strength or weakness of organized labor?					X		X		X		X	
What are the human resource strengths and weaknesses of the company?	X	X	X	X	X	X	X	X	X	X	X	X
How are the various levels of management compensated?	X	X	X	X	X	X	X	X	X	X	X	X
Have there been any major changes in manager compensation within the past two years?			X				X		X		X	X
Are the critical functions staffed with qualified people?	X	X	X	X	X	X	X	X	X	X	X	X
What types of policies does the company have in identifying key management backup positions?						X				X		
Are there cohesive lines of authority and communication?	X	X	X	X	X	X	X	X	X	X	X	X
What is the strategy for filling key positions?	X	X	X	X	X	X	X	X	X	X	X	X

POTENTIAL SOURCES

Intelligence Questions	Sales	Marketing	Finance	R & D	Production	Facilities	Personnel	Planning	Legal	Purchasing	Senior Management	Data Processing
What training programs and apprenticeship systems are used by the company?							X				X	
Does the company have any problems with equal employment opportunities?							X		X			
Are there equal employment opportunities for managerial positions?	X	X	X	X	X	X	X	X	X	X	X	X
How would you compare the salary and wage benefits to that of the industry?							X				X	
Does the compensation plan retain top quality personnel?	X	X	X	X	X	X	X	X	X	X	X	X
What is the current status of labor morale?				X	X		X					
What are the recent trends in employee turnover?							X					
What are the employee turnover rates by function for the last two years?	X	X	X	X	X	X	X	X	X	X	X	X
Have former employees moved into any specific industry or company?							X				X	
To which competitor has the company lost the most key personnel within the last two years?							X				X	
What are the plans to respond to skill or technological obsolescence?				X	X		X				X	
Is there a blend of youth and experience?	X	X	X	X	X	X	X	X	X	X	X	X
What problems exist with OSHA and EPA regulations?					X	X	X		X			

POTENTIAL SOURCES

Intelligence Questions	Sales	Marketing	Finance	R & D	Production	Facilities	Personnel	Planning	Legal	Purchasing	Senior Management	Data Processing
When do major labor contracts expire?					X		X	X	X		X	
What labor negotiations are pending within the company?			X		X	X	X	X	X		X	
What labor unions represent workers at the company?			X		X		X		X		X	

Appendix G

Cases For Telephone Interviewing

Case 1

A business manager has asked you to find out the status of a new product that has been introduced by a competitor. Specifically, he wants to know when it was introduced and what the sales to date have been. The business manager needs an answer by 5:00 pm. It is now 3:30 pm. What should you do?

Step 1: List potential sources of information.

Step 2: Because of the time constraints, rank the sources as first, second and third.

Step 3: Assuming you call the company directly, list potential people you might call.

Step 4: List the questions to be asked regarding the introduction date and the sales to date.

Step 5: Determine possible objections to your questions.

Example Solution

Step 1: List potential sources of this information.

■ Conduct a quick data base search

■ Call internal people
  —sales and marketing
  —operations
  —engineering
  —research and development

■ Call external people
 —trade associations
 —securities analysts
 —industry consultants
 —customers
 —suppliers
 —the competitor

Step 2: Because of the time constraints, rank the sources as first, second, third, etc.

■ Conduct quick data base search

■ Call internal people

■ Call the competitor

Step 3: Assuming you call the competitor directly, list potential people you might call.

■ Customer Service

■ Technical Information

■ Public/Investor Relations

■ Librarian

■ Senior Secretary

■ President or General Manager

■ Other Senior Executives

Step 4: List the questions to be asked regarding the introduction date and the sales to-date.

■ "I have an interest in your product. Can you tell me a little bit about it?"

■ "I'm surprised we haven't heard about this product!"

■ "I bet this product is doing extremely well in the marketplace!"

■ "Is that hundreds or thousands? Closer to_____or_____?"

■ "These sure must be priced right!"

Step 5: Determine possible objections to your questions and a strategy for overcoming the objections

Objections	Strategies of Overcoming
■ "Who are you?"	■ "I'm John Smith", or ■ Ignore the question
■ "What company are you with?"	■ "XYZ Corporation" ■ Ignore the question
■ "Why do you want to know great about this product?"	■ "I've heard a lot of things about it!"
■ "We can't give out sales information."	■ "Is it doing better or worse than the previous product?"

The example interview for this case is in Chapter 4.

Case 2

Company of Interest: Acme Medical
Large medical products manufacturer

Background:

The company of interest is a major competitor in your market segment. Your company's field sales force has reported that the competitor is experiencing several backorder and manufacturing problems. Accurate information pertaining to the cause and scope of these problems is crucial in defining any relative advantage your company may hold over the competition.

Research Questions:

■ What is the source of the reported backorder problem?
■ How long are the manufacturing problems expected to last?
■ Does the problem center around technical, manufacturing or labor difficulties?
■ What are the competitor's perceived losses?
■ Has the competitor identified the solution?
■ How many products are being affected?

Potential Non-published Sources of Data:

- Customers
- Competitor's sales representatives
- Competitor's technical service representatives
- Competitor's public relations representatives
- Competitor's operations manager
- Competitor's production manager
- Competitor's director of marketing
- Competitor's distributors
- Security analysts
- Trucking companies

Representative Interview With a Customer

Interviewer: "Hi, how are you? My name is Pat Allen and I'm calling to find out if you have had success with Acme's medical product." (rapport building)

Interviewee: "Yes, we have used it in the past but not lately. We haven't been able to obtain it."

Interviewer: "Oh, really. What do you mean?" (open-ended question)

Interviewee: "Well Pat, in the last few months, we have been told it has been on backorder. They say they have had trouble maintaining the product's stability."

Interviewer: "Have they mentioned when they expect to have the problem cleared up?" (direct confirming question)

Interviewee: "They don't know quite yet. It's a manufacturing problem that hasn't been solved."

Representative Interview with the Competitor

Interviewer: "Hi, this is Pat Allen. I have some questions about one product that you manufacture. Can you help me?" (rapport building)

Interviewee: "I'll try, what questions do you have?"

Interviewer: "I was speaking to a friend who recommended your medical product. He stated that he hasn't been able to obtain it lately." (Suggestive Statement)

Interviewee: "Recently we have had problems maintaining the stability of our product."

Interviewer: "Stability of the product?" (restatement technique)

Interviewee: "Yes, we found the quality control values for this product vary widely. We have found it difficult to work with the new organic compounds."

Interviewer: "I see. Do you think you'll have the problem solved in a couple of weeks or by the end of the year?" (bracketing technique)

Interviewee: "Probably not in the next few weeks, but we should be back on track within six to eight weeks."

Interviewer: "You must be glad it has just affected this one product." (statement to elicit a response)

Interviewee: "These new compounds have caused problems in other products."

Interviewer: "Which ones?" (open ended question)

Interviewee: "Our line of patient-related medical products."

Interviewer: "I see." (statement to elicit a response)

Interviewee: "But we expect to clear these problems up when the initial organic compound situation is solved."

Representative Interview a Second Source Within the Competitor Company

Interviewer: "Hello, this is Pat Allen. I just spoke with Terry Williams in Technical Services." (rapport and credibility)

Interviewee: "What can I do for you?"

Interviewer: "I had a question concerning your medical products. When will these products be available again for sale?" (direct confirmation)

Interviewee: "These products should be available again sometime in the next six to eight weeks."

Interviewer: "O.K., thanks for your help."

Interviewee: "Any time!"

Case 3

Companies of Interest:

Several major pharmaceutical drug firms.

Background:

Several major pharmaceutical firms have the potential to develop a product which could compete directly with a product that your firm is currently developing. You need to know which competitors are in the process of developing a product and when those products will be available.

Research Questions:

■ Which company is developing a similar product?
■ When will the product be introduced in the market?

Potential Non-published Sources of Data:

■ Local Pharmacists
■ Research Physicians
■ Director of Research
■ Security Analyst
■ Investor Relations
■ Customer Relations

Representative Interview with a Security Analyst

Interviewer: "Hello, I'm Pat Allen. I am interested in finding out who is currently involved with specific drug projects." (rapport building)

Interviewee: "There are several major firms involved in this area."

Interviewer: "Who?" (direct question)

Interviewee: "Well, there are several. Give me your address and I'll mail you a list."

Interviewer: "O.K., but I would really like to know one or two firms who would be involved." (statement to elicit a response)

Interviewee: "I've heard Corporation X and Corporation Y interested in those areas."

Interviewer: "Thanks for your help; this will surely give me a start."

Representative Interview With Competitor 1—Director of Research

Interviewer: "Hello, I'm Pat Allen and I am interested in a specific drug." (rapport building)

Interviewee: "What type of questions do you have?"

Interviewer: "What is your opinion of the specific drug application?" (open-ended question)

Interviewee: "We don't feel there is much potential for development of such a project, at least given our resources."

Interviewer: "What do you mean?" (open-ended question)

Interviewee: "We don't have any plans for a project but I've heard Corporation Y is working on it."

Interviewer: "Do you know anyone in Corporation Y who is involved in this project?" (direct question)

Interviewee: "No, I don't know anyone specifically."

Representative Interview with Competitor 2 Director of Research

Interviewer: "I'm trying to reach the Director of Research."

Interviewee: "This is he."

Interviewer: "This is Pat Allen and I have an interest in a specific product. Would you know if there are any companies working on this type of product?" (rapport building)

Interviewee: "That's an interesting question. In fact we are involved in work in that area."

Interviewer: "Oh?" (open-ended question)

Interviewee: "We have just started to explore different properties which hold potential."

Interviewer: "Properties which hold potential?" (restatement technique)

Interviewee: "We feel that this basic product can be processed into different forms such as tablets and capsules."

Interviewer: "Interesting! It's amazing how far companies in this field have progressed. When do you think such a product will be available to the public?" (direct question)

Interviewee: "Oh, I'm sure it will be a long while."

Interviewer: "A long while?" (restatement technique)

Interviewee: "Well yes, we estimate it could be available in 18 to 24 months."

Appendix H

Competitor Profile Checklist

I. The Company

Present legal name.

Address and phone number of main office.

Type of business.

Description of business activity.

Changes in business activity.

Date of company origination.

State of incorporation.

States where allowed to do business.

List of subsidiaries or divisions.

Addresses of all facilities.

List of shareholders if privately held.

Number of shares owned by principals.

List of types of securities.

Number of shares outstanding.

Number of shares in float if publicly held.

Price range of stock if publicly held.

Stock sales volume if publicly held.

Number of shares authorized.

Number of shares of treasury stock.

List of other operating investments and amount.

List of any unusual situations or circumstances.

Name, address, phone number of company advisors.

II. Historical Summary

How company was originally formed.

Reason for founding.

Names of founders and successors.

Brief review of sales progress.

Brief review of profit progress.

Brief review of product line history.

III. Management, Personnel and Policies

Number of employees by department.

Organization chart.

List of officers.

Information on principals and key employees.

Indication of strength of secondary management.

Indication if management will stay if there is a change of ownership.

Rates of compensation for management.

Outside consultants used.

Description of morale.

List of fringe benefits to management.

Production labor (if manufacturing).
1. Average hourly rate.
2. Names of unions.
3. Past labor relations.
4. Present or future labor problems.
5. List of hourly rates and job classifications.
6. Payroll procedures.
7. Productivity experience.

8. General employee morale.
9. Procedures for hiring and firing.
10. Union contract expiration dates.
11. Number of hours in work week.
12. Advancement and promotion procedures.

Employee benefits.
1. Incentive plans.
2. Pension plans.
3. Vacation plans.
4. Number of paid holidays.
5. Medical, life insurance, dental.
6. Stock options.
7. Bonuses.
8. Profit sharing.
9. Recreation facilities.
10. Employee discounts.
11. Employee social functions.

IV. The Facilities

Land and buildings.
1. Location and zoning.
2. Legal description and ownership.
3. Mortgages (amount, terms and conditions).
4. Description of lease(s).
5. Appraisals (if owned).
6. Condition.
7. Repairs needed.
8. Improvements.
9. Amount of square feet in buildings.
10. Amount of square feet of land.
11. Amount of rent.
12. Amount of property taxes.
13. Amount of office space in building.
14. Amount of warehouse space.
15. Number of shipping docks.
16. Type of electrical power.
17. Compliance with OSHA.
18. Compliance with Environmental Protection Agency.
19. Space for expansion.
20. Location of public storage facilities.

21. Plans for existing facilities.
22. Alternative sites.
23. Property costs.
24. Is location desirable.
    a. Labor
    b. Marketing
    c. Shipping
    d. Materials
    e. Transportation
25. Production and sales capacity of facilities.
26. Percentage of use.
27. If retail facilities —
    a. Approximate size of trade areas
    b Demographics of trade areas
28. Location of nearest:
    a. Post office
    b. Airport
    c. Rail
    d. Port
29. Service by common carriers and United Parcel.

Equipment.
 1. List of equipment: age, date purchased, cost, stock number, condition.
 2. List of tooling, dies, jigs, fixtures.
 3. Obsolescence.
 4. Depreciation policy.
 5. Value of all equipment.
 6. Own vs. lease.
 7. Adaptability for other operations.
 8. Ability to resell.
 9. Maintenance costs.
10. Replacement costs.
11. Layout.
12. OSHA compliance.
13. Other regulatory compliance.
14. Equipment safety.
15. Equipment parts policy.
16. Noise pollution conditions.
17. Preventive maintenance policy.

V. Production (If Manufacturing)

Production costs.
1. Labor cost as percent of sales.
2. Material cost as percent of sales.
3. Manufacturing overhead as percent of sales.
4. Possible improvements and economics.
5. Future cost prospects for labor, material and manufacturing overhead.
6. Production costs and profits by product.

Production procedures.
1. Production schedules.
2. Flexibility.
   a. Flexibility to increase and decrease production.
3. Minimum production required for breakeven.
4. Efficiency of assembly procedures.
5. Percent of product purchased outside.
6. Quality control and inspection.
7. Salvage policy.
8. Efficiency of material handling procedures.
9. Production obstacles.
10. Maximum production capacity with existing equipment.
11. Type of cost controls.
12. Inventory control procedures.
13. Frequency of physical inventory counts.
14. Time studies.
15. Lead time.
    a. How long?
    b. Can it be reduced?
16. Other types of controls.
17. Coordination between sales and production.

Engineering, research and development.
1. R&D cost as percent of sales.
2. Number of employees.
3. Market research program.
4. List of patents, copyrights, trademark, and all new applications.
5. Patent agreement with employees.
6. Patent licensing arrangements.
7. Is current R&D budget sufficient to maintain the company's competitive position?

VI. Marketing and Products.

Product lines.
1. List of principal products.
2. If retail or distribution:
   a. Identify suppliers.
   b. Exclusive arrangements/contracts.
   c. Length of the relationship.
3. Use and application.
4. Brochures and price lists.
5. Comparisons:
   a. Estimated sales and profits.
   b. Nature of trade practices.
   c. Price comparisons.
   d. Packaging comparisons.
   e. Utility comparisons.
   f. Value comparisons.
6. Seasonality
   a. Seasonal characteristics.
   b. Other available products to round out season.
7. Pricing:
   a. Effects of increases.
   b. Stability of prices.
   c. Future pricing considerations.
   d. Fair trade laws.
   e. All price lists.
   f. Bidding conditions.
   g. Should prices be increased on some products?
   h. should prices be decreased on some products?
8. Completeness of product line.
9. Effect of general economic conditions on product line.

Sales.
1. Breakdown by product last 5 years.
2. Breakdown by product next 5 years.
3. Methods of distribution:
   a. Changes being considered.
   b. Coverage of markets.
   c. Elimination of markets.
   d. Direct sales.
   e. Methods of obtaining distributors or deals.

f. Specific areas covered.
g. Loyalty of customers:
   1. Is there a big turnover of customers?.
   2. What is the nature of reorders?
h. Use of private brands.
i. Other methods of distribution being considered.
j. Sales to original equipment manufacturers.
k. Customer attitudes.
l. Effect of franchising.
m. If retail:
   1. Should more store be opened?
   2. Should some existing stores be closed?
   3. What areas or stores?
   4. Credit policies.
   5. Sales department.
4. Sales force information.
   a. Number of employees and organization chart.
   b. Sales methods.
   c. Percent of sales to top 5 customers.
   d. List of top 20 customers and sales volume.
   e. How salesmen are paid.
   f. Types of sales incentive programs.
   g. Nature of sales expenses.
      1. Should they be increased or decreased?
      2. Can existing profit margins afford changes?
   h. New business.
      1. What is being done to get it?
      2. What percent are new customers each year?
   i. How will existing customer sales be increased?
   j. How will average order be increased?
   k. Special promotions.
   l. Policy on service and returns.
   m. Sales forecasts.
      1. Are sales forecasts and budgets kept current?
      2. How accurate have they been?
   n. Does the company know where it wants to be in 5 years? How can it reach that goal with existing program?
   o. How does the company develop new products?
   p. Is proper use made of telephone?
   q. Are sales people making best use of time?

r. Government business.
   1. Is company getting its share of government business?
   2. How can present program be improved?

Advertising and sales promotion
1. Name and address of advertising agency.
2. To what extent does it do its own advertising.
3. Is present agency doing a good job?
4. Is advertising budget on target?
5. List of advertising media.
6. What is dollar amount of advertising budget?
   a. As percent of sales?
   b. Breakdown of budget for magazines, newspapers, trade directories, mail order, phone directories, radio, TV, trade shows, special promotions, premiums.
7. Is a steady public relations program maintained?
8. Does the company make use of testimonials?
9. How often does a publicity release go out?
10. Is company image and logo right?
11. How many trade shows are attended?
12. Is advertising program ready for a new theme?
13. Are mailings made at lowest rate?
14. Are customers and potential customers being followed up as part of each campaign?
15. Are results of advertising being measured?

VII. Financial

Current financial statement.

Financial statements past 5 years.

Summary for past 10 years.

Average profit for past 3 years—dollars and percent of sales.

Average profit for next 3 years—dollars and percent of sales.

Projection for next 5 years.
1. Sales and profits
2. Cash flow

Dividend policy and record for past 5 years.

VIII. Legal Considerations

State and local laws.
1. States in which incorporated
2. States in which qualified to do business
3. Local restrictions
4. Shareholders
   a. Number of voting shares required to merge
   b. Dissenter's rights
   c. Notice requirements
   d. Pre-emptive rights
5. Board of Directors—actions required in corporate sales, purchase, or merger
6. Mergers
   a. Restrictions with respect to foreign corporations— domestic corporations
7. Negotiating permit requirements
8. Requirements and exemptions for registration
9. Requirements and exemptions to give proper notice
10. Bulk sales laws
    a. Compliance requirements and exemptions
    b. Penalties
11. Consumer laws and considerations
12. "Fair trade" considerations
13. "Right-to-work" labor laws
14. Zoning laws and restrictions

Federal laws.
1. Anti-trust laws
   a. Sherman Act
   b. Robinson-Patman Act
   c. Clayton Act
   d. Federal Trade Commission rulings
   e. Department of Justice rulings
   f. Court rulings
   g. Company's past and present anti-trust history
2. Anti-pollution laws
3. Labor laws
4. Other regulatory agencies
5. Tariffs and quotas
6. Securities & Exchange Commission requirements
7. Government contracts

Outstanding contracts.
1. With suppliers
2. With subcontractors
3. With customers
4. With unions
5. With distributors/franchisees
6. With government
7. Contingent or implied contracts

Labor considerations.
1. Union rights
2. Pensions
3. Safety and working conditions
4. Minimum wage
5. Maximum hours
6. Overtime
7. Child labor
8. Discrimination—racial and sex

Patents.
1. License agreements
2. Trade secrets
3. Trademarks
4. Copyrights
5. List of patents with numbers
6. List of patents pending

Appendix I

Listing of Potential Data Base Elements

This appendix contains the results of a brainstorming session on bottom-up data base development. This illustration is not intended to be a complete list nor is it the suggested answer. It shows that a comprehensive data base covering all customers, competitors, suppliers and industry events can be a very significant undertaking. The bottom-up approach needs to be tempered with judgement; the data base should focus on information that is, or will be, strategically relevant.

Account Class
Actual Calls
Actual Contribution
Actual Cost
Actual Expense
Actual Marketing Costs
Actual Price
Actual Profit Contribution
Actual Selling Expense
Average Amount of Sale Over Time
Amount of Sales Over Time
Budgeted Amount of Sales Over Time
Forecasted Amount of Sales Over Time
Average Delivery Time
Customer/Market Class (A,B,C)
Customer Name
Date of Last Call
Direct Fixed Manufacturing
Direct Labor Hours
Distribution Costs
Dollar Sales Quota

247

Fixed Distribution & Sales
Fixed G&A
Fixed Overhead—Actual Cost
Forecasted Marketing Costs
Forecasted Profit Contribution
Freight Costs
Gross Margin
Gross Sales
Sales by Industry
Sales by Region
Inventory Dollar Value
Inventory Location
Item Warehouse Cost
Labor—Actual
Labor—Estimated
List Price
Major Customer Names
Margin Amount
Material—Actual Cost
Maximum Miles Shipped
Advertising Methods
Number of Customer Complaints
Number of Customers
Number of Damage Occurrences
Number of Employees
Number of Orders
Number of Service Calls
Number of Units Sold
Number of Units Sold Over Time
Order Entry Costs
Order Quantity/Receipt Quantity
Other Costs
Other Direct—Actual
Other Direct—Estimated
Other Fixed Manufacturing
Overhead—Actual
Overhead—Estimated
Percent Dollar Volume on Backorder
Planned Calls
Planned Margin Amount

Planned Unit Sales Over Time
Potential Sales Volume
Pounds Shipped
Present Price Breakeven Volume
Product Line Descriptions
Product Sizes (common)
Profit Contribution
Projected Annual Usage
Projected Unit Volume
Promotion Costs by Type
Promotion Type, Content
Quantity on Hand
SIC Code of Customers
Sales District
Sales Region
Sales Territory
Salesman Call Plan—Actual Calls
Salesman Call Plan—Planned Calls
Salesman Name
Salesman Earnings
Service Area of Salespeople
Number of Service Individuals
Service Type
Ship Mode
Bulk vs. Packaged
Standard Delivery Days
Target Inventory Level
Trade Channel
Trade Class
Unit Price
Unit Sales
Units Shipped
Units Sold
Variable Manufacturing
Variable Overhead—Actual Cost
Variable Sales & Distribution
Warehouse Locations
YTD Turnover

Appendix J

Example Security Audit Plan

	MEANS OF GATHERING DATA	INFORMATION RECEIVED	INFORMATION SOURCE
CUSTOMER	■ Contacting customer service and asking a wide variety of questions	■ New product plans ■ Product pricing ■ Product unit sales ■ Product discounts ■ Back order problems	■ Customer service representative ■ Technical service representative
	■ Contacting R&D manager and stating you have to speak to him per territory Sales Representative	■ R&D progress and future products ■ R&D priorities ■ Number of R&D employees ■ Budget for R&D	■ Director of R&D ■ R&D supervisor ■ R&D specialist ■ R&D technician
PURCHASING AGENT	■ Requesting specifications on new or future products from sales, marketing, R&D, or manufacturing	■ Details on new and future products ■ Lead time to new product introductions ■ Confirmation of R&D product/design activities ■ Size and make-up of distribution network ■ Q.C. levels in manufacturing	■ R&D staff ■ Marketing staff ■ Customer service ■ Manufacturing staff
JOB CANDIDATE	■ Direct interviews with personnel, marketing and top management	■ Sales figures ■ New product plans ■ R&D activity ■ Corporate strategies ■ Corporate tactics ■ Company documents ■ Number of employment shifts	■ Personnel ■ Marketing ■ Top management ■ Secretaries

	MEANS OF GATHERING DATA	INFORMATION RECEIVED	INFORMATION SOURCE
JOURNALIST	■ Phone or personal interview with top management for an article, book or trade industry	■ Corporate goals ■ Top management views ■ Top management background ■ Strategic goals ■ Sales and profit figures ■ Forecasted sales and profits ■ Perceived competition ■ Future capital investment	■ Top management ■ Public relations ■ Marketing director ■ R&D director ■ Chief financial officer ■ Plant manager
VISITOR REQUESTING PLANT TOUR	■ Direct observation of administration, manufacturing, R&D and MIS operations	■ Square footage ■ Type of manufacturing equipment used ■ Type of R&D equipment and operation ■ Number and percentage of employees ■ General business operations and philosophy ■ New product information ■ Condition of assets ■ Degree of automation ■ Overhead costs ■ Various company documents	■ Public relations ■ Personnel ■ Manufacturing staff ■ Secretaries ■ Top managers ■ R&D staff
POST AS A SECURITY OFFICER	■ Direct observation of the entire plant	■ Actual throughput on machines employed ■ Scrap ratios ■ Internal documents ■ R&D research projects ■ Quantity of output shipped ■ Production process used	■ Production employees ■ Quality control employees ■ Direct inspection ■ Internal reports ■ Security supervisors ■ Managers ■ Cleaning staff

	MEANS OF GATHERING DATA	INFORMATION RECEVED	INFORMATION SOURCE
DIRECT SURVEILLANCE OF BUSINESS PROPERTY	■ Looking in plant windows ■ Sitting in lobby ■ Walking in halls	■ Obtainable documents ■ Valued "garbage" ■ Number of buildings ■ Age/quality of assets ■ Number of employees	■ Secretaries ■ Security guards ■ Employees ■ Direct inspection
PURCHASING MANAGER	■ Requesting information for vendor company history ■ Requesting information on new vendor management team ■ Requesting information for a review of new vendor financial health	■ Sales figures ■ Total amount of assets ■ Summary of legal action pending ■ Large accounts of the firm ■ Cost of goods sold ■ Operating margins ■ Sales figures by product line ■ Amount of long-term debt ■ Number of employees ■ Names and background of top management staff ■ Corporate highlights ■ Corporate future expansion plans	■ Public relations ■ Marketing ■ Personnel ■ Top management ■ Financial officers ■ Customer service ■ Management secretaries
STAFF ACCOUNTANT	■ Phone requests for financial, marketing and R&D expenditures	■ Sales by product line ■ Cost of goods sold by product line ■ Order backlog ■ Test markets ■ Marketing budgets ■ R&D budgets & expenditures ■ Payrolls ■ Capital investment plans	■ Other accountants ■ Marketing staff ■ R&D staff ■ Personnel staff ■ Operations staff

	MEANS OF GATHERING DATA	INFORMATION RECEIVED	INFORMATION SOURCE
DUN & BRADSTREET REPRESENTATIVE	■ Request for financial and company data ■ Request for top management profiles and new product releases	■ Sales, profits, expenses ■ Number of employees ■ Background of top management	■ Top management ■ Personnel ■ Public relations ■ R&D managers
ACCOUNTANT	■ Phone requests to production foreman	■ Production in units ■ Production per shift ■ Scrap ratio ■ Raw materials cost ■ Current cost overruns	■ Production staff
	■ Phone requests to shipping department	■ Units shipped by product ■ Units returned ■ Truck lines used ■ Number of finished goods received	■ Shipping department staff
INSURANCE COMPANY DATA MANAGER	■ Request for the resubmission of data from company which was lost when computer crashed	■ Detailed summary of all insured employees ■ Detailed valuation of all insured capital assets ■ Summary of future expansion	■ Personnel records ■ Accounting department records ■ CFO department
POSE AS "PLANT CARE" CONTRACTOR	■ Inspecting offices of top management and upper & middle managers	■ Sales ■ New products ■ R&D activities ■ Various internal documents	■ Desks ■ Windows ■ Floors ■ Shelves ■ Files
POSE AS CLEANING STAFF	■ Cleaning and dusting all areas in offices	■ Documents on desks ■ Documents in unlocked files ■ Garbage ■ Audio tapes ■ Overhearing employees	■ Desks ■ Files ■ Shelves, Windows ■ Microfilm ■ Employees

	MEANS OF GATHERING DATA	INFORMATION RECEIVED	INFORMATION SOURCE

SALES REPRESENTATIVE	■ Conducting a sales call	■ Corporate secrets
		■ Corporate rumors
		■ New corporate decisions
		■ Profits, Sales, Employees
			■ Purchasing agents
			■ End users:
			  R&D
			  marketing
			  finance
			  plant maintenance

TEMPORARY EMPLOYEES	■ Daily interaction with internal documents	■ Any sensitive data in
		  marketing
		  finance
		  R&D
		  product
			■ Verbal
			■ Internal documents

INDEPENDENT CONSULTANT	■ Requesting information in a specialized way and later in a specific manner over a wide range of topics	■ New product plans ■ Sales, Profits ■ Units sold ■ Competitive benefits ■ Marketing strategies ■ Acquisition strategies	■ Financial staff ■ Marketing staff ■ Public relations ■ Top management
FINANCIAL ANALYST	■ Phone interviews with top managers who have access to information	■ Future business plans ■ Financial projections ■ Profits, Sales ■ Personnel changes ■ Insight to strategic plans ■ Industry overview ■ Future mergers & acquisitions	■ Divisional managers ■ Departmental managers ■ Top management secretaries ■ Lower level supervisors
STUDENT	■ Phone interviews to gain information of academic projects	■ Corporate structure ■ Corporate location ■ Sales by product/division ■ Budgets as a percentage or in dollars ■ New product concepts	■ Young educated employees ■ Top management ■ Secretaries ■ Division managers ■ Staff accountants

	MEANS OF GATHERING DATA	INFORMATION RECEIVED	INFORMATION SOURCE
CUSTOMER	■ Contact with firms who are known subcontractors of services or goods for the target firm ■ Personal meetings work better than telephone discussions—can state that you were referred to the subcontractor by the target firm	■ Recent projects which are just starting or just completed ■ Key decision makers at firm ■ R&D, marketing budgets ■ Capital investment budgets	■ Subcontractors ■ Managers who work with subcontractors ■ Accountants who paid for subcontractor services and goods
IRS STAFF	■ Request to resubmit the various financial and tax data to IRS office	■ Capital investment data ■ Details of net operating performance ■ Details of employee files ■ Previous year tax return	■ Staff accountants ■ Chief financial officer ■ Accounting clerks

Appendix K

Detailed Action Plan

I. Establish Need for Function

I-1. Review the company's strategic plans, organization charts and monthly management reports. Identify major strategies and areas of emphasis. Identify primary users and providers of information.

I-2. Identify key competitors (current and potential), products/ services, customers, markets and technology.

I-3. Assess relative competitive strengths and weaknesses.

I-4. Identify the competitor that represents the biggest threat.

I-5. Answer the questions "Why business intelligence?" Define business intelligence and its relationship to the overall strategic management function of the company.

I-6. List the potential benefits of a more coordinated approach to this function.

I-7. Outline the overall approach to the development of this function.

I-8. Approximate the incremental cost of developing this function as well as the ongoing costs.

I-9. Meet the potential "champions" within the organization to sell the concept.

I-10. Determine if senior management approval is necessary.

II. Identify Reporting Requirements

II-1. Determine industry success factors.

II-2. Translate industry success factors into key control indicators.

II-3. Determine the bases upon which your company competes in the marketplace:
—price
—differentiation
—focus
—other

II-4. Define types and levels of reporting:
—news bulletins
—competitor profiles
—strategic impact worksheets
—executive intelligence briefings
—situation analyses
—special intelligence briefings
—others

II-5. Determine frequency of reporting:
—daily
—weekly
—monthly
—quarterly
—as required

II-6. Determine key users of intelligence:
—senior management
—line management
—staff management
—salespeople
—other

II-7. Develop preliminary report formats with "live" data from one key competitor.

II-8. Discuss reports with potential users and solicit suggestions for enhancement.

II-9. Refine report formats based on discussions.

III. Identify Data Requirements and Sources of Information

III-1. Review reporting requirements and identify data required.

III-2. Further develop internal network of individuals that will provide intelligence.

III-3. Identify knowledgeable industry sources for your external network.

III-4. Develop a call sheet (consisting of name, affiliation and phone number) for the internal and external networks.

III-5. Call each name on the call sheets and ask them for their ideas on sources of information.

III-6. Review directories of on-line data bases to determine which ones may be applicable to you:
—"Supermarkets"
  —Dialog
  —Nexis
  —Newsnet
  —Other
  —Industry specific data bases
  —Financial data bases
  —Dun & Bradstreet
  —Compustat
  —Other

III-7. Review directories of business information.

III-8. Contact trade associations.

III-9. Arrange for clipping services.

III-10. Discuss findings with library personnel and augment your list of potential sources.

IV. Gather Data and Prepare Prototype Reports

IV-1. Begin to gather data for one key competitor.
  —clipping services
  —on-line data bases
  —internal and external networks
  —other

IV-2. Begin to develop manual filing system.

IV-3. Prepare a complete set of reports for one key competitor and issue regularly for a period of two to three months.

IV-4. Discuss reports with users to determine satisfaction level and determine changes to be implemented.

IV-5. Implement changes and review with users after a two to three month period.

IV-6. Begin to gather data for other key competitors.

V. Finalize Staffing Requirements

V-1. Determine primary tasks to be performed.
—gathering information via telephone from internal company personnel
—gathering information via telephone from external company personnel
—reading and summarizing clippings
—performing on-line data base searches
—interacting with internal company personnel in the interpretation of information
—analyzing information for strategic and/or tactical significance.
—preparing periodic reports
—presenting findings to management
—responding to ad hoc inquiries

V-2. Estimate time required to perform each task for each competitor.

V-3. Estimate time frame in which the intelligence function will be developed.

V-4. Determine mix of part-time and full-time personnel required based on time phasing:
—initial data gathering and analysis
—ongoing activities

V-5. Determine background that full;-time candidates should have based on relative percentages of time for each task:
—business or technical degree
—company experience

—planning experience
—marketing experience
—financial experience
—systems experience
—research experience
—communication skills;—written and oral
—motivation, enthusiasm and other factors

V-6. Estimate number and type of personnel required as well as associated costs.

V-7. Review staffing requirements with management.

V-8. Screen internal candidates.

V-9. Screen external candidates.

VI. Determine Approach to Mechanization

VI-1. Develop evolutionary approach to mechanization:
—word processing
—PC data base
—PC spreadsheet
—interface to mainframe computer
—more sophisticated fourth generation approaches

VI-2. Review reports previously designed.

VI-3. Review manual filing system.

VI-4. Develop tentative data base design:
—top down
—bottom up

VI-5. Develop checklist of software requirements.

VII. Design and Install Mechanized System

VII-1. Review software alternatives.

VII-2. Select software and hardware.

VII-3. Finalize report design based on software capabilities.

VII-4. Finalize data base design.

VII-5. Code, test and debug the system.

VII-6. Build the data base.

VII-7. Develop procedures.

VII-8. Produce first set of mechanized reports.

Appendix L

Business Intelligence Books and Reference Sources

Almanac of Business and Industrial Financial Ratios. Troy, Leo. Englewood Cliffs, New Jersey: Prentice-Hall, 1985.

American Statistics Index: A Comprehensive Guide and Index to the Statistical Publications of the U.S. Government. Washington, D.C.: Congressional Information Service, 1973.

America's Corporate Families: The Billion Dollar Directory. (annual). Mountain Lakes, New Jersey: Dun's Marketing Services.

Annual Statement Studies. Philadelphia: Robert Morris Associates. Updated annually.

Business and Economics Books and Serials in Print. New York: R.R. Bowker.

Business Information Sources. (revised edition, 1985). (Lorna M. Daniells, author). Berkeley, California: University of California Press.

Business Information Sources. Lorna M. Daniells. Berkeley, California: University of California Press, 1976.

Business Intelligence: Methods for Collecting, Organizing and Using Information. Sammon, William L., Kurland, Mark A. and Spitalnic, Robert. New York: John Wiley & Sons, 1984.

Business Organization and Agencies Directory. Anthony Kruzas and Robert C. Thomas, eds. Detroit, Michigan: Gale, 1980.

Business Periodicals Index. New York: H. W. Wilson, 1958. Monthly except July, with periodic cumulations.

Business Serials of the U.S. Government. Richard King, ed. Chicago: American Library Association, 1978.

Business Services and Information: The Guide to the Federal Government. Philadelphia, PA: Management Information Exchange, 1978.

Business Statistics. U.S. Department of Commerce. Washington, D.C.: Government Printing Office, 1932.

Competitive Strategy: Techniques for Analyzing Industries and Competitors. Porter, Michael E. New York: The Free Press, 1980.

Competitor Intelligence: How To Get It—How To Use It. Fuld, Leonard M. New York: John Wiley & Sons, 1985.

Corporate Intelligence and Espionage: A Blueprint for Executive Decision Making. Eells, Richard and Nehemkis, Peter. New York: MacMillan Publishing Co., 1984.

County Business Patterns. U.S. Bureau of the Census. Washington, D.C.: Government Printing Office, 1943.

Current European Directories. 2nd edition, 1981. CBD Research Ltd. Detroit: Gale Research Co.

Directory of American Firms Operating in Foreign Countries. 10th edition, 1984, 3 volumes. New York: Uniworld Business Publications, Inc.

Directory of Corporate Affiliations. Skokie, IL: National Register Publishing. Annual.

Directory of Directories, 3rd edition. Detroit, Michigan: Gale Research Company, 1984.

Directory of Online Databases. Santa Monica: Cuadra Associates, Spring 1985.

Directory of United States Importers. (biennial). New York: Journal of Commerce.

Directory of U.S. Corporations. (annual). New York, New York: Fortune.

Directory of Wall Street Research. (annual). Rye, New York: W.R. Nelson & Company.

Dun & Bradstreet International. Principal International Businesses. New York.

Dun's Business Rankings. (annual). Mountain Lakes, New Jersey: Dun's Marketing Services.

Employment and Earnings. U.S. Bureau of Labor Statistics. Washington, D.C.: Government Printing Office, 1909.

Encyclopedia of Business Information Sources. Paul Wasserman, ed., 4th rev. edition. Detroit, Michigan, 1980.

Encyclopedia of Associations, 19th Edition. Detroit: Gale Publishing Company, 1984.

Europe's 10,000 Largest Companies. (annual). Mountain Lakes, New Jersey: Dun's Marketing Services.

Everybody's Business: An Almanac: The Irreverent Guide to Corporate America. Milton Moskowitz, Michael Katz, and Robert Levering, eds. New York: Harper, 1980.

Exporters Directory/U.S. Buying Guide. 2 volumes (biennial). New York: Journal of Commerce.

Guide to American Directories. 12th ed. Coral Springs, Florida: B. Klein Publications, 1986.

Guide to Special Issues and Indexes of Periodicals. 2nd ed. New York: Special Libraries Association, 1976.

How To Find Information About Companies: The Corporate Intelligence Source Book, Edition III. Washington, D.C. The Washington Researchers, 1983.

How To Win With Information or Lose Without It. Garvin, Andrew P. and Bermont, Hubert. Glenelg, Maryland: Bermont Books, 1980.

Industrial Marketing Research. Cox, William E., Jr. New York: John Wiley & Sons, 1979.

Knowing One's Enemies: Intelligence Assessment Before the Two World Wars. May, Ernest R. Princeton: The Princeton University Press, 1984.

Million Dollar Directory. New York: Dun & Bradstreet. Updated annually.

Moody's Investors Industry Review. (loose-leaf). New York: Moody's Investors Service, Inc.

Moody's Investors Service: Moody's Manuals. New York: Moody's Investors Service, 1955. Annual with semi-weekly supplements.

National Directory of Addresses and Telephone Numbers. (annual). New York: Concord Reference Books.

News Front/Business Trend Directory. Petaluma, California: Ward Publications. Updated periodically.

Predicasts F & S Index Europe. (monthly, with cumulations). Cleveland: Predicasts, Inc.

Predicasts F & S Index United States. (monthly, cumulating quarterly and annually, option for weekly). Cleveland: Predicasts, Inc.

Principal International Businesses. (annual). Mountain Lakes, New Jersey: Dun's Marketing Services.

Protecting Your Business Secrets. Saunders, Michael. New York: Nichols Publishing Company, 1985.

Pugh's Directory of Acronyms and Abbreviations. Eric Pugh, ed. Phoenix, Arizona: Oryx Press, 1982.

Standard and Poor's Register of Corporations, Directors, and Executives, United States and Canada. New York: Standard and Poor's, 1928.

Standard Directory of Advertisers. (Classified and Georgraphical Editions) Skokie, IL: National Register Publishing, 1980.

Standard Directory of Advertising Agencies. Skokie, IL: National Register Publishing, 1981. 3 volumes.

Techno-Bandits: How the Soviets Are Stealing America's High Tech Future. Melvern, Linda. Boston: Houghton Mifflin Company, 1984.

The IMS Ayer Directory of Publications. Fort Washington, PA: IMS Press.

The New Competition. Fahey, Liam, Kotler, Phillip, Jalusupitak, Somkid. Englewood Cliffs, New Jersey: Prentice- Hall, 1985.

The Statistical Abstract of the United States. U.S. Department of Commerce. Washington, D.C.: U.S. Government Printing Office. New abstract annually.

The Top 1,500 Private Companies. (annual). Parsippany, New Jersey: Trinet, Inc.

The Wall Street Journal Index. Princeton, New Jersey: Dow Jones Books, 1958.

The World Almanac & Book of Facts. New York: Newspaper Enterprise Association, Inc. Updated annually.

Thomas Register of American Manufacturers. New York: Thomas Publishing. Updated annually.

Trade Names Dictionary. 4th edition, 1985-86, 2 volumes and a supplement. Detroit: Gale Research Company.

Trade Names Dictionary. Ellen T. Crowley, ed., 2 ed., Detroit, Michigan: Gale Research Company, 1979.

Trade Directories of the World. (annual loose-leaf service with monthly supplements). Queens Village, New York: Corner Publications, Inc.

201 Checklists: Decisions Making in International Operations. New York: Business International Corporation, 1980.

Ulrich's International Periodicals Directory. New York: R.R. Bowker, 1932. Annual.

United States Government Manual. Superintendent of Documents. Washington, D.C.: U.S. Government Printing Office. New manual annually.

U.S. Industrial Outlook. U.S. Department of Commerce. Washington D.C.: U.S. Government Printing Office.

(Year) U.S. Industrial Outlook of 200 Industries with Projections of (year). U.S. Department of Commerce, Trade and Industry. Washington, D.C.: Government Printing Office, 1960.

Value Line Investment Surveys. New York: Arnold Bernhard, 1937-Weekly.

Ward's Directory of 51,000 Largest U.S. Corporations. Petaluma, California: Ward Publications.

Where to Find Business Information. Brownstone, David M. and Carruth, Gordon. New York: John Wiley & Sons, 1982

Who's Who in America. Chicago: Marquis Publications.

Who's Who in Finance and Industry. Chicago: Marquis Publications.

World Directory of Multinational Enterprises. John M. Stopford, John H. Dunning, and Klaus O. Haberich. New York: Facts on File, 1980.

World Wide Chamber of Commerce Directory. Loveland, Colorado: Johnson Publishing, 1967.

Index

A

Action Plan
   Detail, 259,260,261,262,263,264
   Summary, 152
America's Corporate Families—The Billion Dollar Directory, 25
Analysis Techniques
   Business Screen, 79,81,82
   Growth-Share Matrix, 79,81,82
   Industry Maturity—Competitive Position Matrix, 53,54,55
   Macro Analysis, 87
   Micro Analysis, 75,76,77,78,87
Annual Reports, 28

B

Banking Sources, 43,165
Bracketing Technique, 65,66,72
Budget, 140,141
Bureau of Economic Analysis, 34
Bureau of Industrial Economics, 33
Bureau of Labor Statistics, 34
Business Information Sources, 23
Business Periodicals Index, 23
Business Screen, 79,81,82
Business Systems Development, 117,118,119

C

Challenging Technique, 66,72
Clipping Services, 26,27,119,138,141
Competitor Intelligence System, 47,52
Competitor Profiles, 92,94,96
Congressional Research Service, 33
Continuous Monitoring, 3,4

D

Data Base, External 38,39,40,41,42,96,119
   Derwent, 40,42
   Dialog, 38,42,192
   Disclosure, 40
   Dun & Bradstreet, 40
   Electronic Yellow Pages, 40
   Investext, 40
   Moody's, 40
   Newsnet, 38,186
   Nexis, 38,173
   Predicasts, 40
   Standard & Poor's, 40
   Thomas Register, 40
   Trinet, 40,42
   Who's Who, 40
Data Base, Internal, 45,53,125
Decision Support Systems, 126,128,132
Derwent, 40,42
Design, System, 117–132
Dialog, 38,42,195